NOT TOO OLD—
NO LONGER YOUNG

Reflections of a Chaplain

Randall (Randy) Shields

CROSSBOOKS

CrossBooks™
A Division of LifeWay
1663 Liberty Drive
Bloomington, IN 47403
www.crossbooks.com
Phone: 1-866-879-0502

First published by CrossBooks 06/19/2014

ISBN: 978-1-4627-3843-4 (sc)
ISBN: 978-1-4627-3844-1 (hc)
ISBN: 978-1-4627-3842-7 (e)

Library of Congress Control Number: 2014910937

Printed in the United States of America.

This book is printed on acid-free paper.

To the memory of my Mother and Dad, who once were young and now, no longer old! The love they lived, the home they shared, and the sacrifices they made continue to bless me!

CONTENTS

PREFACE

You are not too old to read this book. It is age appropriate!

And since this book is for those no longer young, forge ahead. You, too, are age appropriate!

Think about it. Youth ended for all of us way back there … somewhere. We were newborns. It was our first day of life outside the womb. By the time we left the hospital to go home we were already three days old (not three days young)! The words *young* and *old* are reference points—markers along the road.

For example, when I was in grade school, people would ask my parents, "How's that young boy of yours doing?" But I didn't want to be a young boy. I wanted to be in high school, doing things those old kids got to do, like drive a car and play on the local basketball team. And yet the parents of those old high school kids still considered them to be young. Their children had curfews to keep and homework to do. They were becoming, but were not yet, independent. *Young* and *old* are very fluid, elastic, relative terms.

I am old when compared to my children and grandchildren. But I am considered young (at age sixty-seven) by the residents whom I serve in a retirement community. Their average age is eighty-seven. They regard me as a kid. I think you get the point.

Those young in years (How young is young, and how many years add up to old?) are often restless to become old, while the old (How old in years, and when did it happen?) often yearn to be young again. Add to this mix factors such as the country lived in, the century lived in, race, ethnicity, social status, gender, health conditions, etc., and one-size-fits-all definitions of *young* and *old* become illusive. There are the developmental stages of life. There are the emotional seasons of life. We can use the terms *young* and *old* in self-serving ways. There are so many variables.

But regardless of your age—old, older, oldest—you are not too old to read this book!

And every day you are growing older, so you are no longer young, though you may be younger than some, or in your circle of friends youngest of all!

Not Too Old—No Longer Young is about aging. It's about living. It's about living the gift of life God has given! It's about living as we are, and living where we are.

And where are we? All of us are somewhere between birth and death. We are not too old because otherwise we would be dead, and we are no longer young because we've seen a few birthdays come and go.

The psalmist said it very simply. "I have been young, and now am old; yet I have not seen the righteous forsaken or his children begging bread. He is ever giving liberally and lending, and his children become a blessing" (Psalm 37:25–26 RSV).

So where is this book going to take you? The pages that follow could be considered a collage. The words spread across these pages will be like colors splashed upon a canvas. The collage will introduce you to some people you've not met before. From a distance they may appear to be just a collection of the very old and the rather ordinary; nondescript folks with the colors all running together.

But come closer. Look more carefully. Listen in. There is individuality. Bright hues and soft pastels brush up against one another ... and alongside of us. There are distinctive patterns within the collage. These long-lived people and their heretofore untold stories have much to teach us, if we are willing to learn.

Older folks should never be dismissed as boring or useless. They should never become the forgotten ones or the disposable ones. How demeaning! How insulting! How wrong! They are each special in their own ways. They are unique. They have acquired a wealth of life experience. They could serve as mentors for the many who follow after them, whose life experience is considerably less than their own.

Physically speaking, some seniors are stooped. Most of them are wrinkled. Their hair color, if they still have hair, is primarily gray, mixed-in with shades of silver; and some are dazzling white. Most would not stand out in a crowd, and many would prefer to avoid crowds altogether. Some are into walking to get their daily exercise, while others exercise in the senior fitness room. And then there are those whose exercise consists of lifting the lever on their reclining lounge chair!

Most seniors are neat and tidy dressers. Many like to eat out. Most like to take naps. Many read the newspaper, keeping up with both local happenings and world events.

There are bridge players and bingo players. (Guess which game attracts the largest crowd.) There are movie watchers and baseball fans. Some enjoy crafts. Some surf the Internet. And they all have stories to tell!

In the context of my ministry as a chaplain - a spiritual, caregiving ministry - I'm going to tell some of their stories. I will take you into the world of a continuing care retirement community (CCRC) where I serve. This is a community where a lot of folks are very active in their independent living, where assisted living and memory care are provided when life begins to change, and where a skilled nursing facility—or care center, as we call it—is also located on the same campus for individuals whose health issues have become more serious, requiring 24-7 care.

I have had to pick and choose, but the stories are all true. Perhaps you will glean an appreciation for the women and the men you meet, cracking a smile or shedding a tear. Maybe you will begin to develop a bond with them, and in turn discover something about yourself and how you feel about aging. What does it mean? How are you dealing with it or not dealing with it?

You are going to read stories about people who are living (or they were when I first began writing this a few years ago), and about many who have died. I know them—or I knew them—by their first names. I will only refer to them by their first names. (And when there is a need to preserve a resident's anonymity, I will change the name without altering the story.)

They are my friends. They have let me become a part of their lives. They have touched my life. Perhaps they will touch yours as well.

Finally, this collage needs a frame. The frame will consist of my pastoral care observations, commentary, insights, things I've learned, things I'm still learning, my personal Christian faith beliefs, growth experienced, and ongoing struggles. My reflections as a chaplain frame the collage, a chaplain serving someone like you - not too old but no longer young!

CHAPTER 1

From Campus Ministry to Senior Ministry

I became a chaplain for Lutheran Senior Services based in St. Louis in September 2002. Did the previous sixteen years of campus ministry prepare me for this shift to the far end of the life spectrum, namely a retirement community with memory and nursing care? Yes, it really did.

We can never forecast our future, but God has a way of doing things in our present that will bless our future, and at the time we are blissfully unaware. When campus ministry began, I was pushing forty. When it ended, it was time for it to end. Slowly, imperceptibly yet predictably, it happened. I grew older. Little by little I was crowned with a sprinkling of salt mixed in with the pepper. It was painless. No Grecian Formula for Men on this scalp. I chose the natural, distinguished gray look. I was aging from top to bottom, inside and outside. Aging never takes a time-out!

During my last year on the college scene—all four of my children were now college graduates—I diversified, filling in as the assistant women's basketball coach. (I had played the game but had no previous coaching experience.) What fun! What an adventure! I would do it again in a heartbeat. It slowed my aging process, ever so slightly.

But the unavoidable truth had become unavoidable: The students were remaining the same age, year after year, and I was getting older, year after year! By now I could easily pass as their father. But they didn't need two fathers. And before long I could pass as their grandfather. Oh my, slow down this bus!

Truth be told, I had neither lost my effectiveness nor been made to feel like a relic. It was just a gut feeling. It was time to move on. It was time to pass the baton. The time had come for an ending. The time had come for another beginning. But I had no clue what it might be or what it might look like until the spring of 2002.

That was when a professional friend did a friendly thing. Having asked permission, this friend passed my name along to one of the chaplains she knew at Lutheran Senior Services. My friend knew LSS was in search mode for a new chaplain. She spoke highly of the organization and of the leadership. She thought it would be a good match—their needs and my gifts.

It was not a matter of pulling strings behind the scenes. It was a matter of my friend (herself a chaplain) saying to me, "Let me make you known to someone I know. What they do with the information will be between you and LSS and the Lord."

I had never heard of Lutheran Senior Services prior to this. I had no aspirations to become a chaplain ministering to seniors. Initially I decided, as people say, "to just go along for the ride." I trusted the instincts of my friend, believing that God works through people to accomplish His purposes. Yet I had no sense as to where this would ultimately lead, if anywhere. For all I knew another year of campus ministry lay ahead.

But it was going somewhere. First, there were the phone conversations. Later, there was an interview with the LSS board of pastoral care. This was sandwiched around a two-day visit to the home office and some of the LSS communities in the metro-St. Louis area. It all culminated in July 2002. Lutheran Senior Services extended me a divine call to serve as an LSS staff chaplain. Specifically, I would be serving the community of Hidden Lake located in North County, St. Louis. I accepted the call. Late in August I moved to St. Louis.

So how did campus ministry prepare me for ministry to seniors? I learned quickly that ministry to those in their seventies, eighties, and nineties was not all that different from ministry to those in their late teens and early twenties. It's all about relationships—relationships forged one by one, and one-on-one - relationships built on trust and anchored in love. The formula is simple. Meet people where they are, get to know people for whom they are, and accept people as they are. The formula has nothing to do with age. I'll explain.

Several months into my first year at Hidden Lake, Ruth took me aside. She was an independent-living resident who was skilled at needlepoint, active in worship, and very tuned in to the ebb and flow of our community life. I will never forget what she said to me that afternoon. Looking me in the eye, she extended this compliment: "There is something I've wanted to tell you. I'm really glad you're here. You don't treat us like we are old people. You treat us like—" (There was a noticeable pause.) "Like we are college kids!"

It was an AH-HA moment! I wanted to shout, "Yes!" But instead I just smiled, gently placed my hand on her shoulder, and said, "Ruth, thank you for saying that, and thank you for letting me be your friend!"

I have looked back on that conversation as a turning point. I was no longer on the outside, looking in. From then on I was sure that I had been accepted, that residents were receptive to my ministry, and that I was being grafted into the Hidden Lake community. (Although I did go home that night, wondering whether the college students ever thought I treated them as old people. Oh well.)

This is how I transitioned from campus ministry to senior ministry.

CHAPTER 2

The Booty Lady

Here is the picture. Let your mind pull it up and bring it into focus. Picture the tiny feet of an infant shrouded in a warm pair of booties. Can you see it? Can you feel it too? We've been there and done that! We are in the picture.

Our mother slipped those soft, miniature coverings over our feet years ago. Our little toes, all bunched together, were hidden from sight. A drop-in neighbor looking on might have exclaimed, "Oh, those booties are so cute! Don't you just wish she'd never outgrow them?" But outgrow them we did.

Now there is another picture and another baby. It's our daughter or son whose feet are just as tiny as ours once were. Their booties are just as warm and just as protective. The little legs, still pulled up toward the chest, move in a herky-jerky cadence. Gently you hold the leg just below the knee and with your other hand slide the booty over the foot, repeating the process with the other leg and foot. Then you think, *How cute is that!*

There is just something about babies and booties. I can almost hear the wistful strumming of my heartstrings.

From infant-sized booties, we grow into socks and tennis shoes and dress shoes and sandals and flip-flops. Our feet spread out and stretch out. Footwear in all shapes, sizes, and colors becomes a big business. But if I still want to wear booties, at which store do I shop, and which aisle should I go down? Will there be a Memorial Day sale on booties? Will a new style of booties be coming out this fall?

I try to make it clear to the salesperson in the shoe department, "No, I'm not looking for bed slippers. I want a new pair of booties. They feel so good on my feet. You can slide across a hardwood floor in them. You can wear them to bed to keep your feet warm on a cold night. Booties are wonderful! Where can I get a pair?"

Helen's Story

The booty lady! She was the go-to person for booties. Her name was Helen, but she was fondly referred to by her friends and the staff as the booty lady! That's how she introduced herself to me the first time we met. "Honey, I'm the booty lady. I just love to make booties. I'll make a pair of booties for anyone. Just tell me what color the yarn should be, and I'll do the rest."

Well into her eighties, she was amazing! Attached to her walker was her sewing bag.

Wherever she went, she knitted booties. Not scarves, not shawls, not mittens, and not hats. Only booties.

She knitted all sizes—small, medium, or large. She knitted for feet that were tender, for feet that were calloused, for young feet, for old feet, and for feet with gnarled toes or protruding bunions. The condition of the feet did not matter to the booty lady.

If Helen had had a professional calling card listing her name, phone number, and address, I can easily imagine it looking like this: There would be pictured a ball of yarn and a pair of knitting needles, and centered beneath them would be the phrase, "Have yarn, will knit. I care about soles!"

Helen's tote bag was always bulging with yarn, balls of yarn, and an extra supply of knitting needles. Knitting booties was her great love. She could be sitting in the community room. She could be socializing in one of our lounges, or she could be relaxing in her apartment by herself. Whatever the setting, it was like God had said, "Let there be knitting," and Helen responded, "Here I am. Send me. Send me!"

Helen did not like to watch TV. She was not a reader. She didn't care to play games or do other kinds of group activities. She just wanted to knit. It was her passion, and she passionately pursued it!

Why booties? I never asked her. She might have said, "Why *not* booties?" In a world of designer jeans and fashion statements, where glitzy magazine covers herald the latest in women and men's apparel, when was the last time you heard a marketing pitch for something so simple as handmade, colorfully designed, adult booties?

For all of her skill and dexterity, I don't think Helen's booties would have ever taken the footwear industry by storm, creating a fashion wave of the future. And for that matter, Helen wasn't out "to make it" in the marketplace. She just wanted to give away booties to people who would wear them.

Helen was not a moody, booty lady. If people didn't want a pair of her booties, she took no offense. She was not pushy. She would not insist that you take a pair. She thoroughly enjoyed knitting booties for their own sake. But she did want them to be worn, so she enjoyed even more giving them away.

Helen did not tag her booties with her name. There were no identifying marks. The booty lady was not about personal recognition. Yes, she gained a reputation in our small community as the booty lady, but that just sort of happened.

I was drawn to Helen. In her own unique way she stood out without ever standing out. She was a plain-looking woman—a no-fuss-no-muss sort of person. When I would compliment her work or tell her how impressed I was with what she was doing, she would deflect it and say, "Oh, honey, I'm just doing what I know how to do and like to do." Cancel her fifteen minutes in the spotlight. Her time would be better spent knitting.

The more I got to know Helen, the more candid she became with me. She would sometimes vent her frustrations about residents whom she regarded as the whiners or the complainers, people who expected to be catered to or entertained. "I don't understand why people have to be like that," she would say, as her needles continued to turn yarn into booties.

She could be brusque. She could be impatient. But she would never put her needles down just to have a conversation. She knitted while she talked, and she knitted when she wasn't talking. I don't think she ever tried to knit and eat at the same time. (There are limits to multitasking.) But given her dexterity, if anyone could have pulled that off, it was Helen!

I have no idea how many booties Helen knitted over the years before she died, and I'm sure she didn't keep a running count. She just kept the booties coming and going—hundreds and hundreds and multiples of hundreds. I have a pair of blue ones myself. My children and their spouses all got a pair for Christmas, my first at LSS. Initially there was some amused laughter when the wrapping gave way to the booties—like a reaction to a joke-gift. After all, booties are for babies!

And then I told them the story of Helen, the booty lady, and her labor of love. I told them how her face lit up when I said I wanted seven pairs for my family. Their amusement became appreciation, and the gift became personal. They never met Helen, but each of them transferred through me their expressions of thanks. And she smiled the biggest smile from ear to ear when I told her.

What I Learned from Helen

Some people struggle to find purpose in life, especially as they age. I hear it often. "I don't have a reason to live. There's no purpose in my life."

I ask them, "What's your passion? What do you love to do? Reclaim it. Keep doing it, even if you can't do it as well as you used to. Or could there be a new passion in your life just waiting to be discovered? Have you ever thought of trying . . . ?"

Everyone needs purpose/passion in their lives, or else as they age, they tend to give up.

The God who created us created us to be creative and to be fulfilled. We need to help one another become creatively passionate. We need to stretch, or to be stretched, in order to find purpose and to experience fulfillment, regardless of our age.

Helen never lacked for purpose. She was just herself—the woman God made her to be. She was the booty lady, and her comfortable booties spoke volumes!

CHAPTER 3

Roller Skates (Blades), Walkers, and Wheelchairs

I remember my first time at a roller rink. I was in awe of the music, the lights, and the soft whirring sound of so many wheels spinning round and round on the hardwood floor. Most of the crowd seemed to know what they were doing, whizzing past me, weaving inside and outside, around the various skaters.

Meanwhile, I was tentatively clinging (for dear life) to the outside rail. I had but one objective. I was determined not to fall. But the goal would not be met. Seconds later I went sprawling to the floor, landing unceremoniously on my butt!

Scrambling to get up before someone ran over me, the wheels came out from under me again. Perched now on both hands and both knees, I had given up all hope of impressing the girl who sat two rows across from me in seventh grade. What a klutz!

While others were so effortlessly skating backward, I was already looking for the nearest bench where I could recoup my losses and then make plans for my next exciting fall! Roller-skating began as a bruising and humbling experience for me.

The roller rink is a vivid, though distant, memory. Today, the falls that concern me are not my own, but those of the residents whom I serve. It is the stuff of which mealtime conversations are often made.

"I heard John fell last night when he got up to go to the bathroom."

"Did you hear that Mary slipped and fell this morning and they had to call 911?"

"I fell this morning when I stepped off the curb to get on to the van. I didn't get hurt. I was just glad JJ (the van driver) was there to help me up. But it sure did scare me."

It is the dreaded word/experience in a retirement community—fall, fell, falling.

Mildred Fell

I remember New Year's Eve four months into this ministry. Our Tuesday afternoon worship service was ending. There was the benediction, the closing hymn, and a few parting words. People began leaving their chairs, moving around, conversing, and heading toward their apartments. I was just turning my back when out of the corner of my eye I saw Mildred lurch forward.

She fell to the floor with a dull thud. But overriding the sound of the fall was the unmistakable cracking sound. A bone had broken. Mildred had caught the toe of her shoe on the carpet and lost her balance, becoming the storied Humpty Dumpty.

Had I been facing the other way, I might have caught her, or at least cushioned the fall, but I wasn't. It was a sickening sound, and for me it was another first. She lay there moaning in obvious pain. The call for 911 went out immediately. In less than five minutes paramedics arrived, took her vitals, evaluated the situation, transferred her to a gurney, and quickly took her to Christian Northeast Hospital for X-rays and follow-up treatment.

Mildred had broken her hip. She underwent surgery to repair the damage. Hip replacements have become almost a routine surgical procedure, at least among the elderly. Coupled with weeks of physical therapy, Mildred would neither be crippled nor bedridden. She learned to walk again with a walker.

The Nuts and Bolts of It All

Like shopping carts in a grocery store, walkers are just part of the landscape in a retirement community, as common as leaves on a tree. I sometimes joke with our residents who attend my Gospel Teaching class (Bible study). Several of them will park their walkers along the wall and then carefully seat themselves at one of the tables. I look at all of these walkers lined up side by side, and I tell them, "You know, this reminds me of one of those old western movies where the cowboys ride into town and tie their horses up in front of the saloon, and then they all go in for a drink."

To which someone might say, "So does that mean you're the bartender here? What do you have on tap for today? We like our beer cold!" And with that kind of lighthearted banter, another class would begin.

There is what I call the "plain Jane" type of walker. It consists of a simple aluminum frame with two front wheels. Worn-out tennis balls are sometimes cut open and placed over the back legs like a pair of socks.

And then there is what I call the Cadillac version, brightly colored, equipped with hand brakes and fancy wheels, a basket for personal items, and topped off, quite literally, with a seat. If you get tired of walking, then you can take a break and sit a spell at your personalized rest stop. Or if you reach your destination and all the seats are taken, you can just cozy up to the bar with your own bar stool.

I am waiting for a new, competitive event to be introduced at the Senior Olympics. It would be called "Walker Races!" Residents would be trained in the technique of leaning forward at a 45-degree angle (for aerodynamic purposes). They would learn to neatly bunch their hair (or what's left of it) beneath a protective biker's helmet. And they would be encouraged to purchase sure-footed New Balance or Nike running shoes (great for accelerating on the straightaways).

The competitors would of course be taught Walker Race etiquette. Do not bump into your opponent's walker through sideswiping maneuvers. This could cause serious injury and would be a display of poor sportsmanship. No rear-ending tactics would be allowed, especially since most residents only wear one Depends undergarment at a time. A single disposable undergarment will simply not provide adequate protective padding should a rear-ending accident occur!

I can only imagine the breathtaking suspense. "To your mark. Get set. Go! Slow-motion go!" I can see it all now. There's a photo finish and then a celebration party for all participants, hosted by the EMTs and the ER staff at the nearest local hospital. The curfew for the party would be 7:00 p.m.

Seriously, walkers reduce the risk of falls. Fewer falls means fewer trips to the ER and fewer surgeries.

Walkers are like preventative medicine. Walkers provide stability. Walkers assist the unsteady with a greater sense of balance. Walkers become a friendly traveling companion through the hallways or on the sidewalks or wherever a resident goes. They can be folded up like a lawn chair and stored in the backseat or the trunk of a car when someone takes a resident to an off-campus destination. "Have walker, will travel" could be a senior citizen's motto. The young can push themselves around on scooters, but as we age, it can become the season for walkers and wheelchairs.

What a simple concept—a chair with wheels, a mobile chair for the otherwise immobile. Some like to be pushed in their wheelchairs. Others continue to use the upper body strength in their arms and shoulders to get from here to there. And what happened between here and there?

We went from crawling to toddling and then from walking to running. There was dancing and climbing and racing. There were muscular thighs and calves. There was automatic motion; the brain flashing messages through the nervous system, and without thinking, there was this fluid motion of feet and legs, balancing body weight so effortlessly, as we moved ourselves from here to there.

But then came the debilitating stroke. Then came Parkinson's. Then came the breakdown of cartilage in the knee joints. Then came the atrophy of muscle tissue. Then came old age. The progression may be from a cane to a walker to a wheelchair, or there may be no progression. You may be walking one day and sitting in a wheelchair the next. The wheelchair can keep life from becoming stationary, while at the same time it can become a public address system that announces, "Life is changing!"

Will's Story

My friend Will, a World War II veteran, is wheelchair-bound. During the war he saw action on the German front as the United States and its allies steadily advanced eastward. For Will, the advancing was done inside a tank, one of those lumbering armored vehicles that could roll over rough terrain or plow through fencing and other forms of barricades.

As the war neared its end, Germany's surrender only days away, Will was part of a memorable operation. His tank was one of the first to break through the walls of Dachau, one of Germany's most notorious concentration camps. The liberation of those emaciated prisoners, many of them walking skeletons, many others unable to walk at all, left an indelible mark on Will's memory, as you might imagine.

Will told me the story while he was sitting in his deluxe, battery-powered wheelchair-scoter. His eyes became teary. His voice quivered. He got chocked up. He relived his past, and it was as though the drama had just played out yesterday. He wore his patriotism on his sleeve, and he still does. He is fiercely proud to be an American, proud to have served his country in their time of war, and proud to be a US veteran. He carries his emotional wounds with dignity.

When I see Will coming down the hall with that big trademark smile on his face, I give thanks for people like him. As his self-propelled wheelchair moves steadily forward, I envision him seated in his tank. Skilled in its operation, he moved doggedly forward, intent on accomplishing that critical rescue mission.

A Closing Thought

Life in a wheelchair is not life in the fast lane. But is life in the fast lane what life is all about? The wheelchair can be a visual reminder that says, "Slow down. Take time to smell God's roses." Sooner or later, I remind myself, I will have to slow down, or I will be slowed down. Accelerated living cannot be sustained. Better to pace myself, today. Better to do more by doing less, today. Better to take care of myself with balanced living, today. Better to sit a spell, today, and then press on, before there are wheels on the chair, tomorrow.

Yes, the young and the energetic, with a keen sense of balance, can still lace up their rollerblades. Their arms pumping vigorously, they can accelerate down the sidewalk or through the park. Whirling along, gliding along, or leisurely rolling along, the contrast is sharp over against walkers and wheelchairs. There may even be a handful of adventuresome seniors who would dare to put on the elbow pads, the knee pads, and the safety helmet, in order to do some free-as-a-bird rollerblading - more power to them! Those using walkers and wheelchairs can cheer them on, or go to visit them should they fall.

Whether skating, shuffling, riding, or rolling, engage the fluid motion of life as carefully and fully as you can!

CHAPTER 4

Remind Me Not to Forget

This has become a classic expression in the senior living community where I serve: "Remind me not to forget . . ." How many times have I heard it? How many times will I say it? "Remind me not to forget . . ." and everyone gets it. We're a very forgetful community.

None of us are immune to the frustration or to the humor of forgetting. None of us can stand aloof, basking in his or her photographic memory. None of us can shake our head in dismay, confounded that so many others have experienced various degrees of memory loss. Call it what you will—a senior moment, a pregnant pause, a momentary lapse, a memory glitch, or whatever—there is no way around it. It just goes with the territory. Memory loss is part of the aging process.

Stories of memory loss, intended to bring a smile or even a hearty laugh, are worth remembering—that is, if you can remember. (It does help to keep it light, folks.) Maybe you've heard this one. Or maybe you have forgotten that you've heard this one. Either way, I'm going to remind you not to forget. It goes like this.

There was this husband and wife who were both well into their eighties and who still resided in their own home. One evening as they sat in the living room near bedtime, Mary said to John, "I want a snack before I go to bed. Would you mind getting me a dish of ice cream?"

John dutifully said he would get his wife a dish of ice cream, but as he headed for the kitchen, Mary added, "And would you put some chocolate syrup on it?"

Her husband said, "Sure, I'll put lots of chocolate syrup on your ice cream."

And then Mary made another request: "John," she said, "I'd also like a glass of milk."

"I'll be glad to bring you a glass of milk," he said. "I'll be back in just a few minutes."

But then Mary said, "John, you're not going to remember all of that. Don't you think you should write it down?"

Now in a bit of a huff, John called back over his shoulder, "I don't need to write it down. I've got a good memory. Just be patient and I'll bring you everything that you asked for."

A few minutes later John finally returned. He was carrying a tray and on the tray were two pieces of buttered toast, a dispenser of honey, and a cup of hot coffee. John sat the tray down. Mary looked at it, and then she looked at John. There was a long pause before she blurted out, "I told you that you should write it down. Where are my eggs?"

"Remind me not to forget … my doctor's appointment. Is it today or tomorrow?"

"Remind me not to forget ... to sign up for the birthday dinner." "Remind me not to forget ... the van leaves at 9:00 a.m. for Shop 'n Save." "Remind me not to forget ... housekeeping has scheduled my carpet cleaning for this afternoon." "Remind me not to forget ... my hair appointment on Friday."

There are so many things to remember and so many details to keep straight. You know what I mean—all of those ordinary, everyday things like where did I lay my glasses? Where did I put the car keys? Where are my dentures? Where are the stamps? What did I come to the kitchen for? I can't find my prescription. Common household objects are no longer common. Simple routines become complicated. The mind slows down, and organizational skills become cluttered.

Collectively, in our community, we help one another remember, even as we collectively forget. Most residents do recognize that we're all in this together. Myrtle's forgetfulness today could become my forgetfulness tomorrow. Reminders not to forget need to be spoken and received in a genuinely caring way.

Just as "Neighborhood Watch" signs appear in some residential areas, giving notice to a stranger or an outsider that there is a collaborative effort taking place, neighbors are watching out for the welfare of their neighbor's property. In a similar way neighbors, whenever possible, bridge the memory gap by reminding, filling in the blank, or even making light of an embarrassing moment.

If you want to energize a community of senior citizens into action, then all you have to do is announce, "I've lost the keys to my apartment! I can't find my car keys!" It's like sending out an SOS or shooting a flare up into the night sky. A beehive of activity is unleashed. I recall an incident that illustrates the point.

Francis's Story

Our Tuesday afternoon worship service had concluded. Some residents had lingered to visit, while others had begun moving on to other things or were heading back to their rooms. It was then that Frances made the announcement that brought residents clustering around her like she was a beehive. "I can't find my keys," were the words that came from her distressed and agitated voice. Instantly the informal search committee had convened, and the search was on.

Frances was ninety-six at the time. She had been a resident at Hidden Lake for more than twenty years, our senior of seniors! For most of those years she lived with her sister.

Neither of them had married. About three years prior to this her sister died. A very private yet proper Frances—proper in the way she carried herself, in the way she dressed, in the very neat and orderly way that she kept her apartment—now lived alone.

Frances was very conscientious about exercising. Every morning and afternoon she would walk the hallways of Hidden Lake. Her one serious limitation was declining vision. As punctual as an expensive watch, Frances would predictably be present at our Tuesday afternoon worship service. Yet even with our large print worship book, conveniently positioned on every chair, her macular degeneration (an eye disease) kept her from actively participating.

When she sat down, she would always lay the songbook beside her chair. That's where she said she had placed her keys—on top of the songbook that she had laid on the floor. She was sure of it, and now they were missing. The usually unflappable Frances was very upset!

Agitation had elevated the pitch in her voice, and she sounded frightened when she said, "I can't imagine where they are. I know I

laid them on the songbook when I sat down, and now they're gone!"
A swarm of her remind-me-not-to-forget friends became her safety
net, her caregivers, and her lost-and-found committee.

There was a sofa beside her chair. Someone removed the cushions,
and another probed, reaching as far down as a hand could reach into
the cracks and crevices of that sofa. But they found no keys.

Several scoured the floor. Nearby chairs were carefully searched. A
few folks combed through the rack where the worship books were
kept. Perhaps her keys had become entangled in the spiral binding
and been carried away when the books had been shelved, following
the service. And still there were no keys.

Multiple sweeps were made in and around the vicinity where Frances
had been sitting. A friend asked her to retrace her steps, "When do
you last remember using the keys?"

And another good neighbor told me, before he quietly slipped away,
that he was going to go back to her apartment to see if she might
have left her keys in the door when she came down for worship. The
minutes continued to slip by. Frances, on the verge of tears, became
more upset.

Finally, hoping to calm her, a friend suggested that she just go to the
office and have the office manager open her door with the master
key. Then if the keys did not show up by tomorrow, new keys could
be cut, and the loss would be short-lived. Behind this suggestion
was another thought that had begun to surface. Maybe Frances had
forgotten.

Maybe the keys were in her apartment. The kitchen counter? The
living room table?

After exhausting all possibilities, the friendly search party began to disband. Frances had become a bundle of nerves, but there was nowhere else to look. She kept insisting, like someone under interrogation, determined to stick to her story, that she had laid her keys beside her chair, resting them on top of the songbook. They just had to be there!

I had joined with others in the search for the missing keys. While I didn't want to leave Frances in turmoil, I also needed to move on with the rest of my day. So as I was trying to come up with a polite exit point, something caught my eye. Frances was wearing a white sweater, the kind you can button up the front, but usually it's left open and worn like a jacket. Near her left wrist, barely visible through the mesh of the sweater, I saw what looked to be the groves of a key.

The residents have their room key and mailbox key attached to a softly coiled band. If they choose not to carry their keys in a pocket or a purse, then it's comfortable to carry them, or more precisely, to *wear* them on their wrists. This arrangement makes the keys easily accessible, and they're less likely to be lost. The passing thought had crossed my mind earlier in the search, *Could she have them on her wrist? Had she forgotten?*

Now it became clear. That was exactly what had happened!

Gently I took Frances by the left hand and asked, "What is this underneath the cuff of your sweater?" She put her other hand on her wrist and immediately felt the key on the wristband. There was a gasp of disbelief and then relief. She hurriedly slipped her right hand under the cuff of her sweater, and in an instant the lost had been found. She clutched the keys tightly in her hand.

Frances sat down and began to cry. It wasn't quite like the parable Jesus once told. A woman who had ten coins lost one of them. She swept her house until she found it and then joyfully went to tell all her friends and neighbors that the lost had been found. Frances cried tears of sadness and embarrassment. She had been so sure of herself ... until now.

In reality, the keys had never been lost. Frances had had them on her left wrist the whole time. She had never thought to look in the most obvious place where almost everyone carried their keys and where she routinely wore her keys. Frances cried because she had forgotten. She wept, unable to laugh, because she felt embarrassed in front of her helpful friends. Frances broke down because she understood the painful message. Her memory was beginning to fail. Memory loss had crept into her life. I gave her a hug and said, "Frances, it's going to be okay. I'm glad we found your keys."

As a footnote to the story, Frances is now a centenarian. Her memory loss has continued to erode. She resides in our care center, no longer in need of keys

What Can I Learn?

Remind me not to forget . . . Will someone need to remind you, or to remind me, not to forget? Oh, the reminders and the forgetting! Where does it end? "Help me. I've become so forgetful. I used to be sharp as a tack, and now I'm becoming tharp as a shack."

"I should know your name. Your face is familiar. Have we met before?" the father asks his son.

Could it be the aftermath of a stroke ... or the early stages of Alzheimer's? Years ago it might be said, "He's becoming senile," or one might say, "She's slipping. Will she need to go to the home for the feeble-minded?"

The cause does not matter. The label is irrelevant. The reality is it happens—slowly or suddenly, gradually or relentlessly, but always irreversibly. When memory fades, when memory fails, life changes so dramatically!

Familiar landmarks become foreign objects. Daily routines become a thousand-piece, unassembled, jigsaw puzzle. A burner is left on, and a fire breaks out in the kitchen.

Clothes are put on backward. Personal hygiene is neglected. Special days—holidays or birthdays—pass by unnoticed, unobserved. The framework that brought order and structure to life begins to crack and then crumbles. It is emotionally painful to watch. It is even more crushing to experience. Our memories are not a seamless garment. Over time the stitching begins to pull apart, and the threads begin to unravel.

Beautiful memories have luster and substance, and detail. When easily recalled, they are like a large collection of Precious Moments figurines, displayed in a family room. Each one is a treasure piece. Each one is a gift. Each one is wrapped in love. Together, our memories tell the story of our life; a lifetime of stories.

But then one day it's as if the lady of the house forgets to return. She had kept her home so neat and clean, always so warm and inviting. Early on everything looked the same, still in its place, appearing much the same as it had the last time she was there. Nothing seemed to have changed. House dust is all but invisible at first. Then a week became a month, and a month became a year. The empty house went unattended. The lady of the house had gone away. She was not coming back. The ability to remember had begun to slip away, more and more. It was striking and it was sad.

Now the house smells musty and unlived in, very uninviting. The mantle, upon which the Precious Moments rest, has become thickly layered with dust. The small figures, variously arrayed, are badly in need of dusting. Unattended, and looking so forlorn, they stand as a sad reminder of happier days, days that are gone.

Silently they scream, "Embrace the moments of your life as you live them. Cherish the people, the precious people God places into your life. Caress the times and the places that bring tears to your eyes or laughter to your voice. Every day you are making memories. Gently care for them as long as you can, and as well as you can, before they are layered with dust and they are gone."

Until then, remind me not to forget!!

CHAPTER 5

The Birthday Refrain

Do you remember when you were young, young as in elementary school young? It was a time when birthdays could not come fast enough. If someone asked us our age, we would quickly let them know, "I'm going to be eight," even though we had just turned seven a month ago.

The young can hardly wait to become old. Looking back it seems strange, but there was a time when we were eager to age.

Many of us remember those rite of passage birthdays—reaching the double digit ten, crashing the teenage barrier at thirteen, sliding into sweet sixteen with the jingle of car keys in our pocket, advancing to high school graduate at eighteen, feeling life was as good as it could get at twenty-one—and so it would go.

But as we run out of those rite-of-passage birthdays, we may start feeling older and liking it less. (When does young turn into old?) If someone asks us how old we are, we mumble inaudibly, in a foreign language, under our breath, or we laughingly lock ourselves into "forever thirty-nine." We may even dismiss the question with something like, "I've lost count."

There are exceptions, of course. Like a rare wine that only gets better with age, there are those who own their age as though it were a badge of honor. I remember the clever birthday card that read on the outside, "Don't worry about turning another year older! I heard that birthdays are good for you!" Then you open the card, and it says, "People who have the most birthdays live the longest!"

If you feel good about yourself, if you enjoy life, if there is purpose and meaning to your life, then celebrating another birthday represents more opportunities to give and to share, to love and to care. It's about attitude. It's about mental disposition. Ask yourself, "Am I living life to the fullest, or am I just existing, as time passes me by?" There are people who, for all practical purposes, died when they were twenty-seven, but their heart kept pumping until they were eighty-three.

How sad! There are the ebullient faces of the aging and the grimacing faces of old age.

I have made it a part of my ministry to visit a resident on her or his birthday. I never ask, "So how old are you?" I ask, "So how long have you lived, and how well are you living?"

I want to shift the emphasis from years accumulated to the gift extended. "And by the way, what are you doing with the gift extended? How is life going for you?" Quality of life trumps quantity of life. I come to celebrate with them, God's gift of life to them.

I do not want a birthday to become just another day. It has been my experience that residents in their eighties or nineties sometimes feel like it is just another day. And then I will say to them, "Let there be a shining star on earth's horizon. Let there be a priceless gem in the jeweler's display case. Let there be *you*, unlike any other. May your life be lived to the fullest!"

The refrain that I hear repeated more than any other, from resident after resident, is this: "I never thought I'd live to be this old!" It could be an independent-living resident going full steam ahead at eighty-seven. It could be one of our assisted living residents slowing down at eighty-nine. It could be one of our skilled nursing facility residents, unable to go very far for very long at the age of ninety-one. And with another birthday comes the echo of the refrain: "I never thought I'd live to be this old!"

Sometimes it is said with a spark of amazement. Sometimes it is said with a sigh of weariness. My comeback question, when I'm with residents on their birthdays who never thought they'd live to be this old, is often, "So how old did you think you'd live to be?"

And predictably the response will be, "Oh, I don't know. I just never thought I'd be here this long."

This will often be followed by a litany of their family trees—how old their fathers and mothers had lived to be, their sisters and brothers. It may turn out that they had logged more years than Mom or Dad, outlived their siblings, and just never thought they'd live to be this old. Birthdays and blessings go hand in hand. Birthdays and endings do the same.

Studs Terkle, the newspaper columnist, once opined, "So who wants to live to be ninety? Everyone who's eighty-nine!"

Ruth's Story

I want you to meet Ruth. She moved to the care center after a short stay in assisted living. The initial move to Hidden Lake had been hard on her, leaving her home after living in the same place for more than fifty years. But as her memory issues became more apparent, the care center became the necessary next step.

I visit Ruth often. She smiles broadly when I knock on the open door and enter her room. She welcomes conversation. We have modified versions of the same conversation every time we are together. Ruth is ninety-one, and she never thought she would live to be this old.

Ruth has three children—a son in Texas, a daughter in Wisconsin, and another son who lives in the area. She tells me the same things each time—where they live and what they do. She tells me about the Lutheran school she attended when she was growing up.

She couldn't tell me what she had for breakfast, but she remembers the name of her school and her teachers. She's proud of how much she learned about the Bible during those years. She is also aware that she has become very forgetful, and she excuses herself.

"I guess when you live to be my age, you can't be expected to remember everything. I never thought I'd live to be ninety, but I guess God isn't ready for me yet. He must still have some work for me to do. I don't know what it is. I guess He'll tell me. I never thought I'd live to be this old." (Now her eyes start tearing, and she reaches for a tissue to wipe them.) She continues, "When you get to be this old, you can't do all the things you used to do. I think God understands. I try hard, but when you get to be ninety, it's just not the same. God must have some purpose for me, but I don't know what it is."

She smiles as she talks. Embarrassing laughter punctuates her monologue. Tears moisten her cheeks. In a sad kind of way she seemed to be saying, "I wish I hadn't lived to be this old." It is not easy getting old when the limitations increase.

Every day Ruth faces a challenge—to find meaning and purpose as she lives out her ninety-second year of life. At the same time she continues to excuse herself. She hides behind her unexpected longevity. She had no idea it would be like this. No one ever does.

Ruth does word puzzles. She joins in group exercise, devotions, and other activities that are meant to entertain and to stimulate. She is not passive. She just never thought she'd live to be this old. A few weeks short of her ninety-second birthday, Ruth died.

She never voiced the question, the question that others raise, and the question that has no answer, "How much longer? How much longer before God calls me home? How much longer will I be here? How near is my end?"

It is only a breath away, a sunset removed, one more game of bingo, one more ice cream social, one more family visit, one more—"And I never thought I'd live to be this old!"

But I am . . . . So, let's celebrate another birthday! "There is a time for everything and a season for every activity under heaven;" (Ecclesiastes 3:1 NIV).

CHAPTER 6

Tribute to a Gentleman

Clarence was a gentleman. It had nothing to do with his manners or his table etiquette or the lost art of standing when a woman enters the room or opening a car door for that same woman (though all of these attributes were his as well). But if that defines a gentleman, Clarence was so much more. Clarence was a cut above. Clarence is what I would call a true gentleman. He was a very wise and gentle man!

I met him on Thursday, September 5, 2002, at one o'clock in the afternoon. I remember the day because it was my mother's seventy-sixth birthday. (I didn't know it then, but this would be her last birthday.) I remember the day because it was my first Bible class with the independent and assisted living residents at Hidden Lake. (Later I would change the name of the class to Gospel Teaching.)

The interim chaplain actually led the class that day. It was my orientation week. I was meeting residents, learning the ropes, getting a feel for this new place where schedules and routines were already in place. I was shadowing the veteran chaplain, observing how things were done, taking mental notes, following her from station to station. Hopefully by the end of the week I could at least give the outward appearance of being ready to take the reins.

I met Clarence in the private dining room. At that time this was the location for the class. He stood out, a rather tall and very dignified-looking man. He wore glasses. He was bald.

He spoke in a clear voice, though it had a bit of a gravely sound to it. But yes, he spoke up! This deserves an exclamation mark! I am highlighting the moment because it has been my Hidden Lake experience that older folks, generally speaking, do little speaking up in a Bible class. They are attentive listeners and willing readers, but they rarely make comments or raise questions.

From day one I knew Clarence was different. He challenged the leader that afternoon with a probing question. When he received, what I would call "a pat answer," well, he just wasn't satisfied. So he followed up with another question. He had an inquiring mind, and he wanted to learn. He always wanted to learn more.

This is how we met. It was the beginning of a friendship, a very dear friendship. I would have the privilege of sharing the last five years and three months of his life. Clarence had already been living at Hidden Lake some five or six years before I came.

He lived alone in a patio home. His first wife died of cancer. He would later remarry only to lose his second wife to the same disease. He spoke of them both in very endearing terms. His first wife was the mother of his only child, a daughter who was now married and living near Kansas City.

The loss of two wives had not left him emotionally paralyzed or in a state of depression. Watching them die, he said, had been the hardest thing he had ever done. But Clarence never felt sorry for himself. He continued to live his life to the fullest.

Clarence was active in the United Methodist Church. His local congregation was only a short drive from Hidden Lake. For many years he served as a Sunday school teacher, and he was an enthusiastic member of the choir. I can only imagine how well his bass voice blended in with the four-part harmony of those Sunday morning choral selections.

And yet to speak of him as an active member of his church is to miss the real point. Clarence did not just put in his time and go through the motions of playing church. Clarence loved his church home. He loved the people who shared his church home and those who confessed the Christian faith with him. He called them "my family." There were times when I heard his voice quiver as he spoke of their love for him and of his love for them. As the hymn writer penned, "Blest be the tie that binds, our hearts in Christian love. The fellowship of kindred minds is like to that above."

Clarence was a gentle man. He was unassuming and soft-spoken. He could laugh at himself or laugh at a good joke. He was the epitome of that sage advice: Do not take yourself too seriously. He didn't! And yet he was very serious about the things in life that really mattered—his relationship with God, his family, and his friends. He had earned respect from his peers. He was highly regarded by those living and working at Hidden Lake; those with whom he ate his meals and shared his time.

Clarence, a man secure within himself, had avoided the pitfall of becoming puffed up with himself. He wore a broad, warm smile that made a person feel comfortable around him, but he was not wrapped up in himself. He was kind without attracting attention. He would always be well groomed. He reminded me of an old pair of bedroom slippers, the kind your feet fit into so comfortably that you would never think of getting a new pair.

If someone from Hidden Lake were to ask me to define the word *dignified*, I would respond, "Didn't you ever meet Clarence Hale?" Clarence personified dignity. The dignity of this gentle man was never more evident than when he contracted Parkinson's disease.

There is no cure for Parkinson's disease. It results in the gradual but inevitable deterioration of the nervous system. There are medications that may slow its progress. There are medications that may afford some respite from its most debilitating symptom—the trembling, the shaking, or the uncontrolled body motion. But eventually those who have Parkinson's will need 24-7 care. They will need assistance with the most elementary aspects of daily life, such as dressing, feeding, and toileting.

Clarence did not live with denial. He did not live with grim resignation, stubbornly determined to keep driving and to live independently no matter what. Clarence knew when it was time to turn in the keys, not only to his car but also to his patio home. He did not wait for people to begin talking behind his back, saying, "Clarence seems to be going downhill lately. I wonder how long he can stay in independent living. Did you notice how Clarence shakes when he's eating? The food keeps falling off his fork."

Clarence was proactive. He made arrangements to move into assisted living. But he was not there long. The tremors increased. Frustration mounted. More care was needed. He then did what many residents at that point resist doing, even fear to do. He chose to move into our care center—the skilled nursing facility at Hidden Lake.

Clarence ignored the stigma that some, regrettably, have attached to living at the care center. The stereotypical images of a nursing home (the way an earlier generation may have experienced it) can generate fear and resistance. Some of those images include old people who are unattended and slumping in their wheelchairs, a distraught woman yelling, "Help me. Help me," but she is ignored. Other images give the impression of long, lonely hours logged in front of a TV screen, eyes glazed, and head sagging, not to mention the disgusting smell of urine that is pungent in every hallway.

But none of these images describe our care center at Hidden Lake. Let me take a time-out from my tribute to Clarence, punch the keypad, and take you inside.

Life Inside the Care Center

Look around. Walk the hallways. Take mental notes. Yes, care center residents do need a lot of care—that's a given. There are residents who cannot see or hear or walk the way they used to. Serious breathing difficulties and coronary diseases are commonplace. Oxygen tanks and plastic tubing are part of the landscape. Many cannot toilet themselves, dress themselves, or feed themselves. They have become like dependent children.

Some residents are afflicted with diseases of the brain. While dementia is a generic term that blankets a wide variety of these afflictions, the most notable and the most talked about is Alzheimer's disease. Reportedly some five million Americans exhibit symptoms of this devastating and still incurable disease. Advancing rapidly in some cases, gradually in others (upwards of ten to twenty years), the results are the same.

Mental faculties deteriorate. Memory loss exaggerates, and someone's mother, father, sister, or brother is left in a world that isolates. Complications from the disease more often than not become the cause of death.

There are residents whose debilitating strokes leave them mildly to severely paralyzed.

Residents may come to the care center because of an injury from a fall, a urinary tract infection, crippling arthritis, or they may have been diagnosed with cancer. The vagaries of old age combined with conditions accumulated over the years can create the perfect storm. It is called "a failure to thrive." The bottom line is that there is a catalogue of health issues that can make living more difficult and nursing care more necessary for the aging.

People die in the care center. But the care center is not a place for people to die. It is not a place for families to conveniently dispatch an aging mother or father, as in an "out of sight, out of mind" approach. No, the care center affirms life. It is the resident's home!

Before you begin looking for the nearest exit, having just remembered an appointment you need to keep, linger a moment longer. There is much more to see and hear. There is vitality in our care center! I am going to say that again ... vigorously! *There is vitality in our care center!*

There is a physical and occupational therapy unit staffed by a team of highly skilled therapists. Their goal is to restore mobility to whatever level that resident is able to reach and to reclaim active-daily-living skills (ADL) for those recovering from surgery, injury, or a stroke. Great things happen there!

The activities calendar is crowded with opportunities. Our staff arranges for quality entertainers to come and interact with the residents—singers, instrumentalists, and storytellers. Residents can enjoy a variety of arts and crafts or an afternoon joyride. Those who are able can go out to eat as part of a chaperoned group. Seasonal parties and special events are scheduled like our annual senior prom.

Leisurely manicures are popular, and so are the weekly worship services and Bible studies that I lead. And the list could go on. This is just a small sample of an even more extensive activity menu.

You can hear laughter, observe learning, and smile at the reminiscing conversations that take place. And it goes without saying, but I will say it anyway. Three very good meals are served daily in a very comfortable dining area. There is life in the care center. It's not a minimal existence.

Residents experience love, and that by itself makes life worth living. God's gift of life does not diminish or lose its value even when the aging process begins to visibly set in—wrinkled faces, brown splotches on the hands and the arms, paper-thin skin, bladders and bowels that have given way to incontinence. God hears the prayer of the psalmist and of the resident, "So even to old age and gray hair O God, do not forsake me" (Psalm 71:18 RSV). The love of God in Christ Jesus creates a caring environment of love.

The care center can only be as good as its caregivers. Diversified skills blend together so that our residents can live their lives to the fullest. Nurses, nursing assistants, medical techs, dietary and housekeeping folks, activity leaders, and social workers—they all work collaboratively as a team. They are trained in specific skill areas, but collectively their focus is on person-centered care. We entrust our residents to care companions. They recognize the individuality of each resident, making it their aim to meet individual needs in a way that maximizes care. It is not a one-size-fits-all approach.

Our care companions, with but few exceptions, are some of the most patient, the most loving, and the most amazing people you would ever want to meet. The residents become their extended family, and that's how they treat them—like family. And like any family setting, a lot of cleaning up and caring for needs to be done. There are dining area messes to clean up, table spills, clothing spills, and food spilled on the floor. There are soiled garments and bathroom messes to clean up. There are bottoms to be cleaned, baths to be given, beds to be changed, and meds to be distributed. Over and over it happens. Again and again it has to be done—repetition, repetition.

There are demanding residents. Patience wears thin. There are hard-to-please residents. Impatience creeps in. Some of them forget to say, "Thank you." Some of them are unable to say, "Thank you." But quality care companions keep on giving and caring. The simple rule of thumb is this: Ask yourself, "How would I want to be treated if I were the resident, if I made the mess, if I could not bathe or dress myself. How would I want my Mother or Father to be treated if they were the resident?"

Occasionally, not often, but I have to be honest, it does happen, there are what I call "mismatched employees." The mismatched are simply not well-suited for this kind of employment, in this kind of work environment. They get a job in the care center, and that's all it is—just a job, a means to an end, a paycheck. The resident becomes an inconvenience. Responding promptly to a call light becomes an interruption. They do just enough to get by.

But unfortunately the resident becomes the victim of this mismatch in terms of how he or she is cared for or not cared for. The resident, for example, may ask to have his or her water mug refilled and hear a gruff response, "I'm too busy now. You'll just have to wait. You're not going to die of thirst." The resident may ask to be transferred from his or her chair to the bed, and in making that transfer the resident is handled roughly rather than gently.

When this mismatch occurs, it has a very negative ripple effect. Family members are impacted when their loved one receives poor care. The care center gets a bad reputation out there on Main Street.

A cloud of distrust forms over the rest of the staff. Team spirit within the staff begins to melt or dissolve. Low morale can set in. Others have to work harder to take up the slack.

This is when administration has to step in. The mismatched employee either needs to be retrained, mentored in basic interpersonal relationship skills, placed on probation and more carefully supervised, or dismissed. The care center is only as good (caring) as its care companions. The old adage is still true and still applies. A chain is only as strong as its weakest link.

The Rest of the Story

When Clarence proactively moved to the care center—and in more than eleven years of experience I have to say, this kind of proactive move is rare—he did not give up on his life. He did not wave an "I surrender" flag. He did not curl up in a corner and wait to die. Clarence modeled what I would call "exemplary aging." He was a shining star to others!

The staff enjoyed his company. Residents, most of whom are women, found him to be courteous, charming, and endearing. This gentle, dignified man, afflicted with Parkinson's, neither complained nor elicited sympathy. For as long as he could, he continued to feed himself, clumsily perhaps, but with resolve. His life was changing, but his spirit did not yield to self-pity. He flowed with the tide and "rolled with the punches."

For Clarence, the care center years were a time when he lived life to the fullest as he had in all of his previous years. I remember them well. He had a private room. He had his reclining chair, his tape player, and his reading machine, a device that would magnify print. He was always a man of contentment.

Clarence selected tapes from an audio library. He was an avid reader/
listener. He especially enjoyed listening to prepared Bible studies and
authors who wrote about the Bible. We often had serious discussions
that arose from what he had heard. He had a probing mind. He
wanted to know more about God and his Word and his ways.
And when he posed some of those why questions, which invite
speculation but usually go begging for exact answers, I would lead
him back to plain and simple Gospel truth.

"Jesus died for you, Clarence. Jesus shed His blood on the cross for
your sins, Clarence," I would say. "Jesus rose again from the dead
for you, Clarence. The Holy Spirit has gifted you with saving faith,
Clarence. When you die, Clarence, your spirit will be with Jesus.
When Jesus returns on the last day, your body will be raised. Your
resurrected body and life-giving spirit will come together again. You
will live forever with Jesus in the place He has prepared for you, the
kingdom of heaven! Clarence, you are so loved!"

Clarence would smile and say, "Yes, chaplain, I believe that. I'm
thankful for what Jesus has done for me. I still have some questions
that I want to ask Him when I get to heaven, but by then I guess
they won't matter," and I would agree. We would talk a bit longer,
and then I would pray with him. He always looked forward to these
visits, and so did I!

The chaplain-resident relationship became a mutual friendship. He
opened up his heart to me. As he aged well into his nineties, he
wanted more and more to leave this life and to be with Jesus. He still
enjoyed his church friends who came to visit, but sensing that his
earthly days were growing shorter, there was still a family decision
that weighed heavily upon him.

Clarence was the father of one daughter. She had given birth to
his only grandson (only grandchild). The daughter, her son, along

with her husband, lived in a suburb of Kansas City. While Hidden Lake had become his home and he had become very attached to the community, he also missed his nuclear family and wanted more time with them, especially his grandson. Several times he would talk to me about this as he considered the pros and the cons of moving or staying. He went back and forth, trying to decide what to do. And then when his daughter told him they would reconstruct their house, adding on an extra room for him with a wheelchair ramp, the decision was made.

In July 2008, there was a bittersweet farewell party for Clarence. It was the day before he moved to Kansas City. His daughter and her family were there. Residents, staff members and friends from his church all came together to express their deep love, respect, and appreciation for this gentle man. He was touched, but then he had touched so many. It would be the last time we saw him.

Five months later in early December, his family brought his body back to St. Louis. He had died a few days after Thanksgiving. The funeral was at his home church. As St. Paul declared, so of Clarence it could be said: He fought the good fight, he finished the race, he kept the faith, and henceforth there was laid up for him the crown of righteousness (2 Timothy 4:7–8 RSV).

He was truly a gentle man!

CHAPTER 7

"You Crack Me Up"

She was a riot!

Pauline resided on the first floor of our care center. Most of the residents on this floor are afflicted with mild to severe memory loss. But that didn't matter. I really looked forward to my visits with her. Let me tell her story and explain what I mean.

Making my rounds through the care center, I often have a generic feeling of "I'm glad to be here again." But there is also a special kind of connection, an unformulated chemistry, something that occasionally develops between me and a resident, and it is much more than a generic feeling. Pauline was just one of those special residents. The chemistry could be hilarious. She was a character!

When Pauline first moved into the care center from independent living, she was one angry camper. (Her nickname was Babe, and she had lived her whole life in St. Louis.)

She was not going to stay in this blankety-blank place—not on your life. There was no doubt in her mind that she could take care of herself. She was convinced she didn't belong in a place like this where everyone had lost their minds or were out of their minds (in her unreserved opinion).

For the first two or three weeks she was like a caged tiger, snarling at everyone who crossed her path. She was like a mini volcano, about to erupt, and at any given moment actually erupting.

Pauline had begun to have some falls in her independent living efficiency apartment.

Memory loss had also become apparent. Her children were convinced that round-the-clock nursing care was needed, and the staff agreed. It was a timely decision. After those early weeks she gradually began to settle in. Well, sort of, but not completely.

Part of the settling in process occurred when a smoking schedule was built into Pauline's day. I think she had smoked since a first-class postage stamp had cost three cents or maybe even longer (perhaps since old Shep was a pup). It may have been her friends who coined the phrase, "She smokes like a chimney." It was a pleasurable pastime for her—like a hobby.

"You've got to get me some cigarettes," she would say as she began to get to know me. "I need a smoke." Early on I took the healthy high road. I tried to talk her out of it. Surgeon General-Chaplain Randy would teach her that smoking was bad for her health and persuade her that she didn't need to put more nicotine in her body.

Wrong! Forget the high road. Forget the moral lectures. Forget the health statistics.

Pauline was a committed smoker. She would remain faithful to her addiction. She would indulge her craving for nicotine. She would blow smoke in your face (if she could) and insist, "You don't know what you're missing. Now go and get me another pack." She had all the answers. Smoking hadn't killed her! She was well into her eighties and had concluded it didn't matter what smoking did to her now. She just liked to smoke. And smoke she did!

You remember the line, "If you can't lick 'em, then join 'em." No, I didn't light up with her. I just laughed with her. When I couldn't find her in her room, I knew one of the staff had taken her outside to the patio or to the flower garden for her morning smoke.

Sometimes I would go out and tease her, "So who are you sending smoke signals to today?" And she would just laugh or come back at me with, "Why don't you join me? The message will get there faster."

Pauline was beginning to come around. There was even a hint of trust. A friendship was developing … from the end of a cigarette! The tiger was in the process of being tamed. The volcano had begun to cool.

Smoking relaxed her. A relaxed Pauline was a fun Pauline. I could pop into her room as I made my morning rounds, and we were sure to have an "off the wall" conversation that would have us both laughing. She would crack me up! It might go like this:

"So, how are you this morning?"

"Oh, I'm down in the back. My back's killing me," she would answer.

"I'm sorry to hear that. Anything I can do for you?"

And Pauline would respond, "Yeah, get me out of this place. It's a nut house!"

I would come back at her, "Get you out of here? Where would you go?"

"I want to go to Chicago," she would say. "Can't you get me out of here?" Flashing her wry smile at me, she would add, "You can pull some strings, can't you?"

"What makes you think I can pull some strings?" I would ask her, trying to keep a deadpan expression.

"Well, you know, you're a big shot around here. You can find a way to get me out."

"Me, a big shot, Pauline? No way. Besides, why would you want to go to Chicago? It's so far away and such a big city. You would get lost up there," I would counter.

"No, I wouldn't get lost," she would reply confidently. "That's where our kids use to play together. Don't you remember?" (She never lived in Chicago, nor did I)

"Oh, yes I remember. You used to return our ball when my kids would leave it your yard after they had been playing with your kids." (Now I'm getting into her imaginary, real-life story.)

"How many kids did you have? I forgot—" she asked.

"Four—same as you," I said.

"That's right," she said, laughing, "They used to have some good times together. We had some pretty good kids, didn't we?"

"Well," I said, "I can't speak for yours, but I know mine were!"

"Oh, yours weren't half as good as mine," she said boastfully.

And so the story would go back and forth, bantering, teasing, turning the trivial into breaking news, and reducing the serious to humorous exchanges—a fantasy world made real while escaping from the real world.

Time and time again Pauline would ask, "Can't you get me out of this place? I don't belong here with all of these crazy people!"

"They're not crazy, Pauline," I would try to tell her, pushing my replay button. "Some have memory loss, and others have lost some of their spark. But they're not crazy."

And her comeback would be, with laughter and twinkling eyes, "Oh, that's a bunch of BS, and you know it!" (Pauline could be delightfully earthy.)

I couldn't keep from laughing with her, but never at her. Political correctness went out the window. There was no thinking before speaking with Pauline. Whatever made it to the tip of her tongue would be flung far and wide, never to be rephrased or recalled!

We had many of those "I want to go to Chicago" conversations. Sometimes I would turn them in a different direction. "So how will you get there?" I would ask.

"If you won't take me, then I'll hitchhike," she would spout back.

"Pauline, you're going to get out there on I-270 and thumb a ride to Chicago?" I would query.

"You bet I will," she would shoot back. "I'm a good hitchhiker. Someone will pick me up, and off to Chicago I'll go. I've just got to get out this place first."

There would be a pause, and then I would say very soberly, eyeball to eyeball, "Pauline, I would really miss you. Life wouldn't be the same around here without you. I don't want you to leave!"

"Oh, you wouldn't miss me," she would say with a brush of her hand.

"Yes, I would. Who's going to tell me how it really is around here if you're gone? Who's going to make me laugh? You wouldn't leave without telling me good-bye, would you? I would really be sad if I walked in one morning and your room was empty and no one knew where you were. And then it would all come crashing in on me. Oh my, she did it! Pauline is hitchhiking to Chicago! She's out on I-270 somewhere, trying to thumb a ride, shaking her pretty little leg out there and trying to get some driver to pick her up. I'll never see my friend again." (And then I would feign deep sadness, even getting my handkerchief out to daub my eyes.)

Now she would start laughing, and I would start laughing. Finally she would say, changing the subject (and she was very good at that), "So what time is your little talk this morning?" (That was her expression for my "good morning devotion" time with residents when I would give my little talk.)

"It's at eleven o'clock. Are you going to be there?"

"I guess so. They're usually pretty good," she would say. Of course she never remembered anything about my little talks, but she would always come, giving me eye contact and her full attention.

And then sometimes I would spin a tale with her. I would say, "Pauline, I need someone to fill in for me this morning. Could you do my little talk for me? I just can't think of anything to say this morning."

She would give me one of those hearty Pauline laughs and then say, "Do your little talk for you? Sure. No way! If they heard what I had to say, they'd never come back again!"

"Oh, you could do it," I would try to nudge her. "The folks get tired of me. You'd make a great fill-in. You would have them eating out of your hand!"

"Forget it," she would say stubbornly but with her wry little smile. "You do the little talk. I'm going to Chicago!"

I wish you could have known her and laughed with her. Pauline was a pistol! She could be a little spitfire! She was earthy at times. She could tease and take some teasing. She loosened me up. Ten lighthearted minutes in her room could make my day.

And then one morning I came to her room, and she was very sick. It happened so quickly. She had chills. She was shaking. She wasn't laughing. The nurse came in, and said 911 had been called. Pauline would be going out to the hospital. I prayed with her, and for the last time we looked into each other's eyes. She died later that day at the hospital before I could see her again.

I was not prepared for such a quick ending. (When will I learn that there is no way to know?) The charge nurse on Pauline's floor at Hidden Lake saw me that evening. She told me Pauline would not be coming back. I groaned. I cried. I grieved. "No, no, it can't be, not yet." I did not want this ending—not now.

I gave to her. She had given more to me. My friend was dead.

For several weeks after her death I could barely make myself go down the hall and walk past her room, knowing it was empty. I did not want anyone else to be moved into *her* room, but of course it has been reoccupied and reoccupied and reoccupied.

I wanted to enter room 123 and laugh with her again. I wanted to play the games we had played. I wanted her to come to one more little talk when I would share a Jesus story and we would sing, "Jesus loves me this I know, for the Bible tells me so."

Pauline cracked me up! I need to laugh more – laugh at myself – laugh at aging – laugh as I age. I am grateful to have known her, and the memories live on!

CHAPTER 8

What's It Really Like Growing Older?

You only grow old by a lifetime of living. And how long is a lifetime? Is it ever long enough?

My youngest sister, Kris, lost her first daughter seven months through the pregnancy. Megan died in the womb and never saw the light of day. Such a short lifetime!

My great grandfather was still smoking his pipe every day when he died at age ninety-four. Most would consider that a very long life!

Every day a person lives, his or her lifetime extends one more day. And every day a person lives, that individual grows older.

Old is what we are for as long or as short as we live. We grow old, and then we grow older. There is no growing young and then growing younger.

Is it to soften the age factor that we sometimes describe a person as young at heart, even though that person has lived many, many years?

We exclaim, "She's eighty-five years young!" Perhaps she is energetic and engaged, but is she really young?

"So how does it feel to be eighty-seven (or whatever age)?" I never ask residents this question. It seems like sort of a nonsense question to me. It's like asking, "So give us the inside scoop. We really want to know: What does it feel like to be alive (after logging eighty-seven long, perhaps hard years)?" And the resident might counter, "So what's it supposed to feel like – this is a new experience for me?"

I wonder to myself, *Is the question inviting an organ recital.* "Tell us all of the aches and pains that have brought you to this aging moment?" Or is the question intended to illicit some kind of profound response, like words of wisdom from the hoary head? For the life of me (no pun intended), I don't know! But please (the only request that I will make in this book), please don't ask me, "So how does it feel to be your age?"

And if you do ask me, then I might just tell you, as I hold one hand to my forehead and ponder deeply, "I can't … I can't … I can't find the words to express it, except to say it is absolutely beyond description. I have never had a feeling quite like it. But should you live this long yourself, then you will know what it feels like, and you will not have to ask these kinds of birthday party questions!"

There are the stoics. They coin expressions like, "Growing older isn't for wimps."

There are the disillusioned. They lament, "It's a lie! Whoever said these were the golden years didn't know what they were talking about. There's nothing golden about these years, and if there is, then it must be fool's gold!"

There are the lighthearted who joke, "You know you're growing old when all of the names in your black book end with the letters MD. Or you know you're getting older when you get winded playing a game of checkers."

And there are the pragmatic who will say, "I don't really like growing older, but when I consider the alternative—"

No one has a choice to stay young or to grow old. Every day I live, I grow older. I am part of a vast movement—all-encompassing, universal in scope. Every day is a growing older day … for everyone!

Often I tell my residents, "I am taking notes. You are my teacher. I want to learn from you. I am watching you grow older. I'm moving the same direction you are. You just got started before I did. You're blazing the trail. I'm traveling on the same road just as others before you carved out the trail and you followed them. I have so much to learn from you. Teach me as best you can."

Older people know so much more about younger people than younger people can ever know about older folks. (The older folks have been there and done that.) The critical difference, of course, is life experience. Younger should be willing to learn from older. Seniors have a reservoir of teaching moments to draw from—their own bad choices, poor decisions, and wasted moments along the way. Seniors have those "if I had it to do over again" stories to tell. The reservoir and the stories could serve a younger generation well.

What is it like growing older? It is the accumulation of life experiences— by the minute, by the hour, by the day, by the month, and by the year. It is the movement of time in the space where we live. What is it like growing older? I can't explain it, but I know it happens. It is happening breath by breath, moment by moment, and most of the time we're not thinking about it. But this is a good time to wonder about it. Let me think out loud with you.

From Mabel I Learn What It's Like

If I were to take my cues for growing older from Mabel, growing older would be like—well, it would be like winning the "Busybody of the Year Award." With a nose so long that it finds its way into places where it does not belong, growing older becomes an intrusive kind of life.

Mabel makes it her business to nose about, telling others what she has nosed out and then adding her own jaded spin to Hidden Lake happenings, not to mention our un- happenings. She likes to submit her reports in *St. Louis Post-Dispatch* fashion, often with a flair for the dramatic. Mabel can create firestorms that scorch innocent bystanders. It is called hurtful gossip or the spreading of half-truths.

My take on it is this: Old age has not generated Mabel's pattern of behavior. Rather, this has been Mabel's sad trademark throughout her life—one that she continues to spit and polish. Is it loneliness driven? Is this her way of getting attention, as in bad attention is better than no attention? This is not how I want to grow older, an unrestrained tongue, dwelling on the negative, and hurting other people in the process.

And so I pray, "Make me a good listener, Lord, and if need be, a tongue-tied listener. The story stops here. My nose is for smelling your roses, not for digging around in other people's gardens. Let me grow older, genuinely caring about others, rather than gossiping about others. Empower me to speak the truth in love. In Jesus' Name. Amen."

From Russell I Learn What It's Like

If I were to take my cues for growing older from Russell, growing older would be like—well, it would be like winning the "Complainer of the Year Award." Very few people can please Russell. After his daughter and granddaughter, the list becomes so short that there is no list. Russell could be perfectly happy when he was completely miserable.

Russell moved here only because of his wife. It was her decision. Had the decision to move been his, he never would have crossed the threshold. After his wife, Lillian, died, he blustered on and off about moving somewhere else or about buying a house and getting out of his assisted living apartment, but it was all bluster. In reality, Russell couldn't find the time to pack up and move. There were too many things to complain about. The food wasn't prepared well. There were no activities just for men, but when activities just for men were provided, he never joined in. "They make you pay too much to live here," he grumbled. He could be such a grump. Efforts to cheer him up or to encourage him to become more positive fell on deaf ears (and no, he was not hard of hearing).

Russell did not begin to hone his complaining skills coincidentally with the move to Hidden Lake. The pattern was well engrained long before he moved here. Whether in the workplace, his home, or other social settings, he made sure people heard him coming before he got there. This is not how I want to grow old, pulling people down or turning people off with my carping comments.

And so I pray, "Lord, awaken me to the beauty that surrounds me— my community, the people who share life with me, the abundance of your blessings lavished upon me. Let me enjoy the wonder of living and the Wow of your handiwork. And should I have complaints that need to be addressed, show me constructive ways to do that without a whining voice. In Jesus' Name. Amen."

From Grace I Learn What It's Like

If I were to take my cues for growing older from Grace, growing older would be like—well, it would be like humbly receiving the "Servant of the Year Award." Grace is such a gem! She is thoughtful and considerate of others. She is a very spiritual woman with a servant heart.

Grace volunteers hours and hours of her time in our care center. She delivers mail to the residents. She visits at their bedsides. She reads Scripture, devotional literature, and stories (full-length novels) to many of her care center friends. She is like a Cub Scout den mother keeping her grown-up little gals and guys, her aging neighbors, well cared for and well loved. This is precisely what she radiates—deep, heartfelt love.

Grace is a regular participant in our weekly worship service and Gospel Teaching class. She has continued to be active in her local congregation. She likes to read good books. She epitomizes our Lutheran Senior Services mission statement, "Helping older adults live life to the fullest" (see John 10:10). Widowed, the mother of four children, a grandmother and great-grandmother, Grace is living her life to the fullest, the same way she had been living it long before she moved to Hidden Lake.

And so I pray, "Lord, let me grow older with a servant heart, not becoming a couch potato, not letting time slip idly away. Open doors so that I may serve others. Let me use the gifts you have given to me for as long as I am able to use them. Give me a passion for living life to the fullest, whether as a chaplain, as a pastor, as a volunteer, as a caregiver, as a trusted friend, or as a loving father and grandfather. May the last years of my life be my best years of life! In Jesus' Name. Amen."

From Elmer I Learn What It's Like

Or I could take my cues for growing older from my dear friend Elmer, where growing older would be like—well, it would be like humbly receiving the "Good Neighbor of the Year Award." Elmer just makes a person feel comfortable around him.

What you see is what you get. He is a no frills, no pretense kind of person who just keeps living life to the fullest the way he's done for more than eighty-eight years (when I was first writing this). If you need a friend or someone to talk to, Elmer will be there for you. He is Mr. Dependable, Mr. Reliable.

Elmer likes to fish. He likes to work with wood. He's converted one of his rooms into a workshop where he can go about his crafty business. He's learned to use a computer, and he likes to be outdoors gardening. He's a handyman, a studious man, a family man, and a widower with four grown children and many grandchildren.

Elmer loves His Lord. Oh, does he love his Lord! And he loves the Word of his Lord. He has several health issues, but he does not complain. He often speaks of his readiness to be with Jesus. A quiet, sincere voice bespeaks the strong faith he has in his Savior, Jesus. He is a friend to many and a pillar in our community. His way of growing older is simply to live older and to live as he has always lived—a faithful servant of the Lord.

Elmer was called home to be with his Jesus in January 2013 at the age of ninety-one. He died in Christ with saving faith. He was ready.

It was a privilege to speak at his funeral. I miss my dear friend very much. He was a great encourager!

And so I pray, "Lord, let me grow older by simply growing older and not letting age get in the way of living. Let me get comfortable with myself as my life changes. Help me to make changes when aging brings change. Let my feet neither slide loosely nor become too snug in my old pair of slippers. Let me live older in spite of those older aches and pains that have a way of slowing a person down or eventually bringing a person down. Let me grow older in a lively sort of way! In Jesus' Name. Amen."

A Closing Thought

I can choose to be a grumpy grouch. I can choose to wilt and then wither away. I can choose to lament and to languish. I can choose to grow older with all the kickin' and screamin' that's left in me, until the zest for living melts into a listless pile of sludge and I become a sorry spectacle of what used to be and could have been. Pain is inevitable but misery is a choice.

Or ... I can choose to age with a gentle heart, alive in the Spirit of the living God, full of His grace in Christ Jesus, with the power of God still at work in me regardless of my advancing age. The psalmist said it so simply and so well, "The righteous flourish like the palm tree, and grow like a cedar in Lebanon. They are planted in the house of the Lord; they flourish in the courts of our God. They still bring forth fruit in old age; they are ever full of sap and green" (Psalm 92:12–14 RSV). Is there a better way to grow old?

CHAPTER 9

The Way It Used to Be

The sitting room in our independent living community is just a few steps away from my office. When I am in my office, I usually leave the door open. The conversations that take place out there can easily be heard, drifting into my workspace.

I am not an intentional eavesdropper. I don't come back from lunch, kick my feet up on the desk, and then settle in for an afternoon of note-taking as I catch up on the latest news from Lake Woebegone, otherwise known as Hidden Lake. But sound waves carry, and for better or for worse, I learn a lot about people and what's going on in their lives.

It is Tuesday morning, and Harry has a doctor's appointment. (Tuesday is Doctors Day at Hidden Lake.) The stage is set for his organ recital, as a captive audience awaits the van that will take each of them to their respective doctors. Perhaps there will be time for others to give their organ recitals, depending on how long Harry's recital lasts.

Dorothy stayed up the previous night to watch the end of the ball game. It had gone into extra innings. Now our resident sportscaster supplies the colorful, play-by-play description of how the winning run was scored. The Cardinal faithful are delighted!

There will be the random query, such as, "So are you going on the scenic ride? How did you like the entertainment at the party yesterday? Did you hear that Herb fell last night? I wonder how he's doing." And so it goes.

But as I recall the bits and pieces of overheard conversations, there is a signature phrase that seems to resurface again and again. I hear it in a more serious, reflective conversation. I hear it when two or three residents leave the present and slip back into their past. I hear it sometimes with a hint of bravado and then again with a trace of sadness. I hear it sometimes spoken with a voice of authority and then again with a wistful longing. The signature phrase is this: "I remember the way it used to be."

The way it used to be. It is such an elastic phrase. It stretches across a lifetime. It weaves its way through decades, pregnant with time. It becomes what I call "a navigating principle," steering the ship in many directions. "I remember the way it used to be."

How It Was for Maisie

Maisie remembered the way it used to be when she grew up as a child in London. She still had her British accent and could tell stories about life on the other side of the pond. She had that dry, English sense of humor, and she would speak in a very formal tone of voice slowly and deliberately, "So, Pastor Randy, how are you today?"

Maisie dearly wanted her life to be the way it used to be. The more she aged, the more she wanted to return to her home of origin. But things would never be the way they used to be. There was no home to go home to. There was no family over there with whom she could live. The way things used to be—they would never be again.

How It Was for Alice

Alice remembered how she used to be a beloved Sunday school teacher in her church. Her face lit up as she rehearsed those days, long since past, when she would share Bible stories with a class of eight or ten children. She also recalled how it used to be when she was a young adult leader on youth retreats. As she remembered how it used to be, you could hear it in her voice and see it in her eyes - she longed to be there again.

Alice had received a twenty-five-year plaque of appreciation from her church for those faithful years of service. Beaming with pride, she showed it to me, and I thought of the refrain from an old hymn: "So I'll cherish the old rugged cross till my trophies at last I lay down. I will cling to the old rugged cross and exchange it someday for a crown!"

But now her church has closed, and the congregational members have scattered or have been absorbed by other congregations. The way things used to be—they would never be again.

How It Was for Ken

Ken used to hunt and fish. He was an avid outdoorsman. He took his family camping when the kids were growing up. He loved to get away to the lake or to the woods or to any natural setting. He could well be described as a true nature lover. I could imagine Ken swapping tales with Daniel Boone, had he lived in that era, or joining a caravan headed west on the Oregon Trail. He would have been the consummate pioneer. "Westward ho the wagons!" he might have exclaimed.

Then arthritis set in. Ken lost his agility. Then there was a fall, and he lost his mobility. But he did not lose his congeniality. He did not lose his sense of humor. He did not lose his faith. He did not lose his will to live. And yet he knew that things would never be the same again. He would never build another campfire or go hiking through the woods or reel in a five-pound bass. Those days were gone—the way it used to be.

How It Was for George and Mary

George and Mary had been Lutheran school teachers. They shared a love for Christian education as well as a love for each other and their four children. But when they moved to Hidden Lake, Mary was already into the mid-stages of what is commonly referred to as Lou Gehrig's disease, a chronic, progressive, severely debilitating disease of the central nervous system. The prognosis is always terminal.

George cared for Mary in their independent living apartment as well as he could and for as long as he could. Gradually she lost her ability to speak, to walk, or to move her arms and hands. The time came when Mary needed 24-7 care. She spent her last days in our care center.

George and his family had vivid memories of the way it used to be. Deep within, they longed for those days to return, yet they continued to show their love and care for Mary, where she was and as she was. The way it used to be would be no more, and it had gone so quickly!

Taking Another Look at What It Means

Nostalgic memories are a good thing. They spark a smile. They trigger laughter. They release a tear. They choke us up. We hold on to the past because we are holding on to our lives. "This is how I lived. This is what we did. This is the way it was ... or at least the way I remember it."

Solomon advised, "Do not remove the ancient landmark which your fathers have set" (Proverbs 22:28 RSV). Ancient landmarks? What are they? Originally the reference would have been to property boundaries—where one landowner's field ended and another's began. But ancient landmarks could have a more comprehensive meaning. Could they not also refer—at least indirectly—to biblical truths and values, as well as relationships passed on from one generation to the next? Do you remember the way it used to be when our way of life was slower, simpler and more wholesome?

"The good ole days" were probably not as good as they are sometimes made out to be. (In literary terms it's called *epic magnification*.) There have always been and there will always be people problems and conflicts of every size and dimension. There is no uncontested, undisputed golden age. But the seniors, among whom I live and serve, remember the way it used to be for them, and so do I.

They remember a more patriotic time when you were proud to "pledge allegiance to the flag" and when singing the national anthem might bring a tear to your eye. They remember when you had neighbors who were friendly, approachable, and accessible and when most people went to church on Sunday. They remember when you did your work first and then played later. They remember when the corner barbershop was a place to catch up on the local news and when the local doctor made house calls but rarely sent you a bill.

They remember when a school incident meant someone was shooting paper wads or had put a tack on the teacher's chair and not that a teacher was attacked in a shooting incident resulting in a school lockdown. They remember when a family might spend an evening in the summer shelling garden-grown peas as they sat on the back porch with Grandma and Grandpa. They remember when they were kids sleeping three in a bed in the upstairs room, a room that held the heat in the summer and the cold in the winter, but family love made it work.

Seniors remember the way it used to be. They took pride in the way they dressed and how they looked regardless of how much or how little they had. Seniors remember the way it used to be. They knew that responsibility went with parenthood and that family togetherness was the way families were meant to be.

Seniors remember the way it used to be. They expected education to bring about learning, and they never would have removed God from the public school or the nativity scene from the public square. Seniors remember the way it used to be. There was virtue in civil discourse, and common sense was not uncommon. Seniors remember the way it used to be. They placed a high value on good craftsmanship, hard work, and a job well done, and they were prudent in their spending.

The way it used to be—No, we cannot live in the past. But we can learn from the past, and we should. We can value the virtues of the past, and we should. We can cherish the people who shared life with us in the past, and we should.

I remember, and celebrate, the way it used to be in rural northeastern Kansas: My roots and my heritage; my faith and my church; the fruit my father raised and the home my mother made; the sweat dripping from my forehead and the cold drink of water quenching my thirst; family games and family devotions; hail storms and wind storms; bountiful harvests and thankful hearts; my first bicycle and the last time I slept in my upstairs room. My cup overflows – more remembering than I can share. It was good, the way it used to be. It was God's goodness in Christ, and that's the way it's supposed to be!

I remember the way it used to be. Do you?

CHAPTER 10

Change?!

Change—it can be a frightening word. It can be an even more frightening experience. It can be a stimulating word. It can become a wonderful experience. Change is unavoidable and inescapable. It is woven into the very fabric of life. Pictures in the family album document that it happens to all of us, like it or not.

Change is happening all around us every day. Flat tires are changed, but there was a time when there were no tires to change, and that in itself bespeaks a whole lot of change. Change in the way we transport ourselves. Change in the way we communicate. Change in the kind of houses we live in and the conveniences that we have come to expect and to enjoy within our homes. Change in the way doctors treat us, hospitals care for us, and the pharmaceuticals that have been made available to us.

And then the child becomes the parent and the parent becomes the child – it can only be described as a season of huge emotional and relational change!

Now there are exceptions, but it has been my observation that the older people get, the less change they want in their lives, and the more difficult it is for them to change.

Seniors like routines and predictability, both of which translate into stability and security.

Do not change the schedule! If dinner has been served at four thirty, then why would you change it to five o'clock? If bingo starts at one thirty on Friday, then why would you change it to two thirty on Thursday? Change the schedule, and you may start an uprising. "If it ain't broke, then don't fix it!" Continuity and consistency carry the day.

Betty's Story

But change often has to do with a bigger issue, namely that of independence and control. My friend Betty, whom I met shortly after I became the chaplain at Hidden Lake, was a frisky independent living resident. We clicked, and her life story poured out. Betty's life had been besieged with change.

Betty and her husband had retired to an Arizona community that provided all of the amenities for senior living. They both enjoyed those years—the climate, the activities, the friends, the whole package. And then he died, and she became a widow in the company of many other widows. She was sad, but she did not feel alone. She grieved, but she was moving on with her life. She had made many friends in this retirement community, her home of choice. And then change was imposed upon her.

Betty's son resided in St. Louis. He thought she should live closer to him. He wanted to be there for her when needed. There was no way I could judge his motives. In fact, as I came to know him later, it was obvious that he genuinely cared about his mother. When she broke her hip and needed to live in the care center, he was there for her, and he was very attentive to her needs. But the decision he made for his mother was insensitive to her needs. The decision to move her from Arizona to St. Louis was a decision of imposed change. As far as I know, the issue was never fully resolved between them.

The change uprooted. The change took her from the comfortable and the familiar, to the uncomfortable and the unfamiliar. She understood what her son was doing and why he was doing it; and yet she had been content in the home she had made for herself, and she had no desire to move.

Betty was losing control of her life. She had no health problems or memory loss. She loved her son, but living closer to him was not high on her priority list. I think she would have said to him (and maybe she did), "If you want to move out to Arizona in order to be closer to me, that would be fine with me, I'll get you in touch with a realtor. You can move, but I don't want to move. I don't want any more major changes in my life!"

With great reluctance, Betty moved to St. Louis. She was angry and upset. At least that's how she told me her story. She lived the last six years of her life as a resident at Hidden Lake. Did she adjust? Yes, she made new friends, one in particular named Esther.

Esther took Betty under her wing. She was a befriending friend, a truly caring friend. She knew Betty's story, her resistance to this move, her longing to return to Arizona, and the stress this had brought into her life. The changing time had not happened easily. But Esther got Betty involved in her church. She introduced Betty to other residents and helped integrate her into this new community.

Betty's story reminds me that change is often a double-edged sword. On the one hand, I may resist it with a passion. I do not, for example, want to lose my right to make decisions independently. But on the other hand, there can come a time and a place and a circumstance when I will need to accept change, albeit reluctantly. And when I do, some good things can happen.

Betty could have sulked or gone into a deep depression when change flooded over her, but instead, with the help of others, (especially Esther) she actually came to enjoy life at Hidden Lake. Perhaps you recall the expression, "When life hands you a lemon, turn it into lemonade!" I know it's easier said than done, but Betty's story says it can be done!

Pat's Story

It seems like it was just yesterday when Pat was out in the living room, working the crossword puzzle that appears daily in the *St. Louis Post-Dispatch*. That's where I would expect to see Pat. That's where her neighbors would expect to see Pat. She was almost ninety-one and still mentally sharp, socially graceful, and fully engaged in the community.

Pat had a ninety-seven-year-old boyfriend. She and Ted would sit together on the sofa, holding hands on movie night, or as she worked a crossword puzzle, he would cozy up beside her, while reading the paper. Romance knows no age limit. Embers left behind can be rekindled.

And then there was change—sudden, dramatic changes in her health. Pat was taken by ambulance to a nearby hospital. She became a patient in the ICU. Five days later she died. She seemed so healthy and looked so good, smiling, friendly, living life to the fullest. She had learned to deal with change. Overnight, as it were, our community and especially Ted, had to deal with change.

Reflecting on Change – It's Personal

Change can bring us to or remind us of finality. The friend or neighbor with whom we often shared a meal and later had a glass of wine to cap off the evening is not sitting at the table tonight. Her funeral is tomorrow. I don't like that kind of change. I don't like the change I see in the mirror—hairline thinning, crow's feet imprinting. I don't like it when I can only watch a basketball game but I can no longer play. I don't like it when the ophthalmologist tells me I need a stronger lens in my bifocals. And I really didn't like it when my dad, before he died, had to be cared for in a skilled nursing facility and wear adult diapers as he became increasingly forgetful. I wanted to scream, "No more change! No more!"

But I know there will be more change, a lot more. Gradually or suddenly it will come. It will surely come! I will lose my fragile world of independence. The car keys will have to go. I will lose control of my life, though truth be told, I have little or no control. The secret—though it need not be a secret—is this: In the midst of change everyone needs to care and to be cared for!

"Does anyone care?" This haunting question, often unspoken, lingers in the air when a resident is facing change, when you or I confront change. "Does anyone care? Does anyone get what I'm going through and what I'm feeling?"

Facing unwanted or difficult change is one thing. Facing it alone, feeling abandoned or forgotten is quite another. A man once said, "When I was twenty-five, I didn't care what other people thought about me. When I was fifty, I cared what everyone thought about me. Now at seventy-five I realize no one thinks or cares about me."

How much do you care? Human touch means so much! It can become the caring hand of God, felt through the hands of others. It can become the presence of God through the presence of another, someone who cares enough to be there, to listen, to pray, to hold my hand, to give me a shoulder hug or a gentle bear hug. To weep with those who weep, and to rejoice with those who rejoice, is to hoist the flag that says, "I care about you!"

But Christians are more than flag-wavers. Christian care embodies the tenderhearted love of God the Father and the compassionate sacrifice of God the Son and the comforting touch of the powerful Holy Spirit. Christians are reflectors, dispensers, and conveyors of His loving touch. Christians are the caring, and we need to be cared for. We all need to be an Esther to Betty. We all need an Esther when we are Betty.

Change becomes less daunting and less threatening when I am not facing it alone, when I am part of a caring community that can say, "We're all in this together." Whether in the role of caregiver or one who is receiving care (and from day to day or week to week, the role itself can change), I am anchored and buoyed by the words of the hymn writer, "Change and decay in all around I see. O, Thou who changest not, abide with me."

Change?!

And so I pray: "We can do this, Lord! It's you and me; it's you and me, Lord! Amen"

CHAPTER 11

Snapshots and Flashbacks: It Becomes Very Personal

Everyone has a story to tell, an experience to share, a moment that stands out.

Our lives become a collage of the incidental and the monumental, of the mundane and the marvelous, of the ordinary and the extraordinary, of the same old, same old, and of the breathtaking and spellbinding.

A camera or a video recorder or some kind of electronic device may capture the special moment—a fragment here or a thin slice there. Oral tradition, written down, or word of mouth, passed along, partially preserves the past. But no album or narrative or chronicle can ever be complete or exact. No one ever steps twice into a stream in precisely the same place.

What has been cannot be relived. The mistakes cannot be corrected. The decisions cannot be remade. The joys cannot be rekindled. The excitement cannot be recaptured. The grief cannot be postponed.

Can you recall when you first said to yourself, or first began to think, *I'm getting old (or older)?* Were you standing in front of the bathroom mirror, the wall fixture that never lies? Were you sitting at the kitchen table, reclining in the backyard, or coming off the tennis court? Suddenly life seemed to be slipping through your hands like a greased pig.

So what should you do? Accelerate and put more pedal to the metal? Splash about wildly in the pool? Write down your bucket list and head for the nearest airport? Put on the brakes, pull off to the side of the road and scream? Make an appointment with a plastic surgeon? Start eating organic food and get on a regiment of herbal supplements? What's next? How do we live tomorrow?

One breath at a time, one moment at a time, one relationship at a time! I ask myself, "Is there more life behind me than ahead of me?" Probably. Yes, I would think so. And it's all out of my hands and beyond my control.

"Remember a simple truth," I tell myself. "The gift of life comes in small packages with an assortment of experiences. Not too much, maybe, and not too little, usually. Not too hard and not too easy. A soft pillow with a hard mattress. An opportunity and a challenge. Take a deep breath and live!"

Champagne fizzes from the bottle. But before I can bring it to my lips, the glass accidently gets knocked off the counter and shatters. Don't cry over spilled champagne.

I baptized my granddaughter late this morning. Earlier in the morning I was at their bedside as two of my resident-friends died. It was a day of bittersweet, mixed emotion.

I relaxed this evening with my favorite author. I wanted to. Tomorrow I have to start working on my taxes. I have to. Such is life.

What a thoughtful phone call I received today. And later I received an abrasive e-mail that left me fuming. Hold on to and let go of and know who you are.

I was able to love our dear residents again today, even though some unloving encounters with nonresidents made my stomach churn. Oh well, sometimes it happens that way.

"Live, Randy," I tell myself. "Ditch the analyzing and pitch the critiquing. Today is the first day of the rest of your life."

Discover blessings hidden in a pile of crap. *Carpe diem!* Tears do not exclude laughter. Expletives deleted can morph into levity exceeded!

The years that I have spent at Hidden Lake, serving as a chaplain, have magnified the truth of God's love for me. They have also intensified this truth for me, "God doesn't make junk!" He tells us in Genesis 1:26–27 (RSV) that He creates men and women in His image.

Still another truth confronts me. I have soiled and spoiled that image by blatant disregard of God's will and by the waywardness of my heart. My human history, and the collective history of all humanity, is a tragic narrative of free will out of control, or as the apostle Paul so concisely said it, "The wages of sin is death" (Romans 6:23 RSV).

But there is good news—good news at its very best! God has rushed to my rescue. Jesus, the Christ, laid down His life for my sins and for the sins of all humanity. My sin will not be charged against me. Punishment will not be extracted from me.

The premier personal sacrifice has been made! Christ, the Lamb of God, shed His blood for me on the cross. "Amazing grace, how sweet the sound, that saved a wretch like me!"

And then Jesus did something that would have been humanly impossible. He took up His life again! He was raised from the dead. The physical resurrection of Christ has overcome death! My worst enemy has met its match. Death cannot do me in. My life had been like a scorched and twisted tumbleweed blowing in the wind, but now I have become a new creation in Christ through the renewing power of the Holy Spirit.

My aging body, inevitably becoming frail with the ravages of time, has already become, as St. Paul declared, the temple of the Holy Spirit living in me (1 Corinthians 3:16 RSV).

Sifting through my rubble, God has graciously chosen me to be His child, or as one of my friends so warmly puts it, "I'm one of the King's kids!"

The beloved apostle John said it so clearly when he wrote, "Jesus did many other miraculous signs in the presence of his disciples, which are not written in this book. But these are written that you may believe that Jesus is the Christ, the Son of God, and that by believing you may have life in his name" (John 20:30–31 NIV).

I have freedom in Christ to live life to the fullest, savoring what has been, relishing what is, and anticipating what will be.

I am not living in a Pollyanna playground, children romping gleefully, everyone imaging that all is well. All is not well. All will never be well in a broken and fallen world.

Someone got it right and said, "I'm not okay, and you're not okay. But that's okay!"

It's okay. I live by the grace God. That means my heavenly Father knows all about me, and because of His Son, Jesus, He loves me just the same! It's okay. I live by grace, through faith in Christ. That means I trust in the saving work of Jesus alone for my salvation! It's okay. I am daily forgiven, daily renewed.

All of my follies and failures, all of my wounds and wounding, Jesus heals. Jesus takes my sin upon Himself. He welcomes me into His heavenly Father's family, the family of the forgiving Christ! And the journey continues. It is always a faith journey.

I am grateful for those with whom I have shared the journey. I am grateful for those whose lives have intersected with mine. Take a look at some of their snapshots and the flashbacks that I've collected over the years. For an instant, it's as though time stood still.

The Florence Snapshot

My friend Florence told me about her father, who at one time had been the personal secretary of Woodrow Wilson. It was fascinating – a president of Princeton University and the President of the United States. I had been connected with early twentieth-century American history through Florence.

The Marian Flashback

My friend Marian had lived in Hollywood when she was a young woman. She worked for a financial institution. Many of the big name movie stars of that era employed its services. Marian helped manage the day-to-day money affairs of the rich and famous, paying their monthly household bills and doing things like that. She spoke of meeting Bob Hope, Gregory Peck, Clark Gable, Jane Russell, Katherine Hepburn and others. She knew them as people and not performers. She knew them as people who were kind and gracious toward her, people who appreciated the service she provide for them. As I recall, Gregory Peck was her favorite. Through Marian, I was connected with a Hollywood that seemed kinder and gentler than Hollywood seems today.

The Ross Flashback

I learned in a small but personal way what it was like to be a black man living in St. Louis before and after the Civil Rights Movement. My friend Ross lived through those years and connected me to them. Even though he scored well on the civil service test and became a mail carrier, he experienced discriminatory practices when he was riding public transportation, had to deal with racial slurs, and felt the rage of some bigoted whites when they found out that a black man was delivering their mail. I cringed with anger at some of the stories he told me. Yet he never spoke with bitterness but always with a courageous spirit.

Diabetes eventually took both of his legs from him. But the disease did not rob him of his faith in the Lord Jesus. An assisted living resident when I first met him, he died in the care center. His African-American story and friendship deeply imprinted my life.

The Gordon Snapshot

I've learned to laugh at Gordon's jokes. He still lives independently at age ninety-eight navigating a bit more slowly with his cane than he used to. He served as president of our Villagers Association. He likes to draw and paint, and he takes part in a variety of activities. He calls a strong game of bingo. At our Tuesday morning coffee and donut gathering, he likes to crack a few jokes.

"You know why Billie takes a ruler to bed with him? Because he wants to see how long he sleeps."

"If you want to kill a squirrel, then all you have to do is climb up in a tree and act like a nut."

"Where do you stand when there's a seasick elephant in the room? As far away as possible." (You saw that last one coming, didn't you?)

"Do you know what the ceiling said to the wall? You're going to have to hold me up. I'm plastered"

The Annie Flashback

And then there was Annie, an African-American woman with a lot of spunk. Annie will not be cited in "Who's Who." She never made a movie or signed an autograph. But she could tell you all about her flower garden and her son, John, a retired St. Louis policeman. She could be rough-and-tough gruff, and she could be a dear! Annie was a resident in the care center when I began my ministry at Hidden Lake. She died five years later. Not only did I lose another friend, but her death also marked a significant passage of time. There had now been a complete turnover of residents at our care center. Annie was the last of what I fondly referred to as "the original thirty-five" (the number of residents living in our care center when I first arrived, nine months after it had opened). And she was an original!

I remember vividly the day Annie was sitting in a chair near the nurses' station. I was having some lighthearted conversation with her. (As her dementia advanced, that became more difficult to do). She got up and started walking to her room, and I quickly sat down. "Thanks for the chair," I said. "You've got it nice and warmed up for me."

She turned and said, "I just farted in it!" I burst out laughing. It was a really warm chair!

The Marie Flashback

I smile as I remember ninety-seven-year-old Marie. (She, too, was part of the original thirty-five.) She was very hard of hearing. She was a devout Roman Catholic. She had never married. She was quite attached to a younger sister, an assisted living resident who would come up to the care center almost every day to spend time with her.

Marie would always be there when I led my good morning devotions, or as I called it then, HUGS (Help Us Grow Strong, Lord). In order to have eye contact with those in wheelchairs, I often do the bended-knee thing, either in a squat position or with one knee actually resting on the floor. Marie's refrain in our devotional circle, when I would speak face-to-face with her and give her a hug, was always, "God bless you, honey." But one morning the unexpected happened.

I was on bended knee. We had made eye-contact. She said her, "God bless you, honey," but it didn't stop there. "And if I were a little bit younger, honey, I would marry you," she continued. It was loud enough to be heard in all directions around the room. (The hard of hearing tend to speak louder.) It was one of those "Oh my" moments! I was totally caught off guard. I could feel myself blushing, and I really didn't know what to say. To this day I have no memory of how I extracted myself from her near proposal.

Yes, I smile when I think of the Marie flashback. I think it taught me that the lovelorn still long to be loved. It also taught me that even appropriate friendship hugs can be misconstrued. A chaplain must always have boundaries.

The Virginia Flashback

The Kansas farm boy in me resonated to Virginia's story. Virginia was raised on a farm in Wisconsin. She was one of fourteen children— fifth in birth order and the oldest of seven girls. She lived the classic generational story of walking two miles, one way, to school every day. The weather did not alter the schedule. The rain clouds could be pouring out their liquid sunshine, or the countryside could be in the grip of a cold Wisconsin winter. Still she and her siblings would make the trek to their one-room schoolhouse.

My friend Virginia recalled mornings when she arrived at school and her hands were so numb she couldn't turn the knob to open the door. She would pound on it with her little fist until someone came to open it. Her formal schooling ended when she finished eighth grade. After that she worked full time on the farm, helped her Mom and Dad, and was big sis to her nine younger siblings. Virginia's story is a small slice of Americana that will never be lived again. I'm glad she connected me to her past. I can see her face and the faces of other friends —so many stories and so many flashbacks, now securely filed away in my memory vault.

The Aurelia Snapshot

There was petite, meticulous Aurelia, who for years and years had been the organist at her Presbyterian church. She was born into a musical family. Her father and two brothers played instruments in their small community band. She proudly showed me their picture. Before she had to move to the care center, she still had a small organ that she played in her apartment.

The Alvin Snapshot

I remember Alvin. He was well into his nineties, all but blind yet still able to hear. He was always there for worship on Tuesday and for Gospel Teaching on Thursday. He was so proud of his son, who had been a missionary in New Guinea. Countless times he would repeat the story of the New Guinea trip he and his wife had taken to visit their son. It was the trip of their lifetime, and they never forgot it.

The Elaine Snapshot

So delightfully I recall dear Elaine. She personified the ever-ready bunny. She just kept going and going and going! She was a friend to all, involved in everything, and the unofficial welcome wagon to every new resident who moved in. Elaine's bubbling personality and contagious smile drew people to her like a magnet. And then quite suddenly she became ill, was hospitalized, and five days later died. Our residents were stunned. How sadly she was missed. I lost one of my cheerleaders and a special friend.

The Harvey Snapshot

I can still see the stately frame and hear the deep bass voice of Harvey, a strong Baptist Christian who loved to sing duets with his wife, Clara, and to teach Bible class at his church. He was a man of unswerving convictions. I had a deep respect for Harvey.

The Matz Snapshot

And I will never forget Matilda. (We all knew her as Matz.) She had been born and raised in India. Her parents were missionaries. She married late in life and never had children of her own. But her stepson became very devoted to her. In her final weeks of life, dying of liver cancer, Earl gave her the love and the care of a natural son.

There are so many ordinary people with unique stories living here at Hidden Lake. All of them were, and all of us are, pilgrims on a journey. Many have ended their journey. Some of us are still on the journey, with time for a few more snapshots and flashbacks.

CHAPTER 12

"If I Should Die before I Wake"

I step outside the door leading to my office. The Hidden Lake LSS logo flag, which is prominently visible in our community, has been lowered to half-mast. It is a silent messenger. A resident has died.

The ambulance from Christian Northeast Hospital arrives on campus. The flashing red and blue lights get our attention. A North County Police car is close behind. The 911 call has gone out, and the community braces itself. Has someone fallen? Will that person need to be checked out? Has someone had a heart attack or a stroke? Was someone found unresponsive in his or her room? Will the flag be lowered to half-mast later tonight or tomorrow?

These are familiar scenes at Hidden Lake. As I write this, nine residents and one colleague have died here in the past month. We have lost a lot of friends and neighbors in a very short period of time. It has been a sobering few weeks, and the entire Hidden Lake family has felt the weight of multiple deaths clustered so closely together.

But Hidden Lake is not a community that lives morbidly, shrouded beneath a dark cloud, waiting pensively for the next siren to sound or for the next funeral notice to be posted. It is not a sullen, sulking community where the most frequent topic of conversation is death. The residents at Hidden Lake are here to live! I am one of their cheerleaders! And this is one of my favorite cheers: "Do as much as you can, as well as you can, for as long as you can!"

Residents are encouraged to keep doing the things they enjoyed doing before they moved here. They are also encouraged to try new things such as art, music, crafts, or games. I want to stimulate their minds, tickle their funny bones (One of my care center friends says I'm a clown.), and touch their spirits. Our staff cares about the whole person. Jesus said, "I have come that you might have life and have it to the fullest" (John 10:10 NIV).

There is a wide spectrum of living that happens at Hidden Lake. Shortly after beginning this ministry, a resident moved into the care center on a Friday afternoon. The next day that person died before I ever met him. And then there are residents who have lived here for more than twenty years. Their roots go way down. They have become my neighbors.

The average life span in the United States is currently 78.1 years. When the twentieth century began (1901), that number was 47.3 years. If life spans continue to lengthen as many predict, then retirement years will also lengthen. The refrain that I often hear from residents goes like this: "My only regret is that I didn't move here sooner." A retirement community of choice is a good place to retire.

Life is good at Hidden Lake. Yes, now and then there are resident issues and staff issues. Conflicts arise. There are problem people anywhere and everywhere you go. But all things considered, it is still a good place to live. There is vitality here. There is energy here. There are engaging people here. There are opportunities to grow mentally, relationally, and spiritually here. There are some very loving and caring people here. There are people who need to be loved and cared for here. And death is here.

I am not always at the bedside when a resident dies. I don't track that kind of thing or keep a log. I don't know how many deaths I've witnessed. But I can tell you it never gets easy. It has never become routine. It is never just another day at the office, one more life-ending moment added to a string of other such moments. I cannot in a stone-faced, professional manner just say a prayer, express my sympathy to the family, and then exit from the room, moving on to other things or to other rooms or perhaps to other deaths. Should I ever become calloused or jaded about death, it will then be time to step away or to retire.

Death is a sacred moment for me. Death is a mysterious moment for me. The miraculous gift of life ends as it began in the womb—in silence. For me it is like standing on holy ground. "The Lord gave and the Lord has taken away," declared Job, "blessed be the name of the Lord" (Job 1:21 RSV).

When the precious gift of life entrusted to Newton, or to Leonard, or to Gladys, or to Luella, or to Dorothy, had run its full course - the chest lifting for the last time, the last breath whispering away - it was a moment of great human loss. A family circle had grown smaller. A friend had taken a permanent leave of absence. They were gone.

Death is not a cookie-cutter experience. If you've seen one, you haven't seen them all. A person, with individuality dies, not an old codger with false teeth, arthritic joints, and splotchy skin, like a lot of other old people. This person was someone's husband or wife, someone's father or mother, someone's uncle or aunt, someone's dear friend. This person had character. This person had talent. This person made other people laugh. This person could do skillful things with her hands. This person reached out to others. This person worked hard to provide for his family. This person was a leader in the community.

But sometimes the person who dies seems to be falling through the cracks and getting lost in the crowd, sadly, like a nobody. Maybe the person was poorly educated, could never seem to get ahead, and had little to show for their life. The person may have had no family or may have outlived his or her family. No one came to say good-bye. No one was there at the end. Who will miss this person? What legacy will this individual leave behind? Did his or her life matter? Will his or her death even make a blip on the radar screen?

The measure of human worth, if measured only by humans, will always be skewed. There is so much more to human worth than meets the eye, so much more than what is squeezed into or left out of the obituary column.

The true measure of human worth is the immeasurable love of God in Christ Jesus. The Lord Jesus loves everyone he has made. Jesus loves everyone he has saved, everyone for whom He died on the cross. Jesus loves everyone for whom He was raised to life again!

In God's divine economy there are no forgotten, unnecessary, discarded, insignificant, or useless lives—none at all! There are only individual persons, people with names, people who have been loved … and forgiven.

Between every first breath, as the wonder of life is embraced, and every last breath, when wonder turns to separation and loss, a story has unfolded. No two stories are alike. In every story the plot gets messed up and the subplot spills out tales of woe, covered over with fanciful excursions to who knows where, and in the last scene there is death.

But there is a compelling twist of irony. These stories are not destined to be shelved and locked away in the dusty archives of obsolete libraries. Every story has been read. Every story has been redeemed. Every character has become the object of amazing grace and unending love. There are so many people who do not know this or believe this. There are so many people who still need to hear this. God the Father has lavishly loved all of us, and all of humanity, through His Son, Jesus Christ.

God is not about opening up junkyards and filling up cemeteries. The God who reveals Himself in the Holy Scriptures is all about tenderness and mercy, "I have redeemed you, I've called you by name, you are mine" (Isaiah 43:1 RSV).

When someone is dying, I want to be there with the person and with his or her family. These folks may or may not believe the Gospel. They may or may not have saving faith in the all-sufficient work of Jesus Christ, their only Savior from sin. They may or may not have repented of their sins. They may or may not have confessed the name of Jesus as their Lord. They may or may not have a childlike faith in the forgiveness of their sins, the resurrection of their bodies, and the promise of everlasting life, with Jesus, in the kingdom of heaven.

The simple Gospel truth is this: God in Christ has done everything for the residents of Hidden Lake (and for you and me)— saved by his gift of grace, through his gift of faith, and not by their (our) works. So at the end of the journey there is either faith, which saves, or unbelief, which condemns - saved forever or lost forever – the glorious home-going of heaven, or the unimaginable suffering of hell, that never ends.

The spiritual condition at the time of death is something I have no control over. But if I can be there when someone is dying, because I care, then I will be. People's lives are valuable!

I have the opportunity to share the Gospel. I have the privilege of sharing my faith, my hope, my love, and my Jesus with the residents of Hidden Lake. Scripture is clear. "God desires all to be saved and to come to the knowledge of the truth" (1 Timothy 2:4 RSV). God and God alone knows what is in a person's heart when he or she dies.

I am a chaplain. I am not the judge. I have been entrusted with a ministry of witness, a ministry of presence, a ministry of comfort, a ministry of compassion, a ministry of caring, a ministry of healing, and a ministry of truth. I serve the living in the midst of their dying.

Hidden Lake is a good place to live. Hidden Lake is also a good place to die. If I were to say this in the public square, most people would not understand. But I can say it on the inside, on the inside of this community, where I live and do ministry, where most just call me Randy, where relationships have been forged, and where we have become for one another an extended family.

I can say it to the residents, "Hidden Lake is a good place to die," and most of them will get it. Most of them will agree, "Yes, this is a really good place to live, and it will be a good place to die."

We can talk about death when it happens. We can talk about death before it happens or when there are those signs that it will be happening again soon. It is not something that we gingerly step around, speak of with hushed voices, in out-of-the-way places. It is a reality. We live with it openly. I can teach about death and the resurrection in Gospel Teaching, and I do. I can preach about death and the resurrection in our Tuesday worship service, and I do. I can laugh about death with our residents, and we do with stories like this one.

A man came home from his doctor's appointment. He was very upset. "What's the matter, dear?" his wife asked.

Her husband answered, "The doctor told me I have to take these pills for the rest of my life."

"Well," his wife consoled, "that's not so bad. Lots of people take medications, and they stay on them for the rest of their lives."

"I know," her husband said, "but he only gave me four pills!"

An interlude for a joke or two has its place. It says in Proverbs that "a cheerful heart is good medicine" (Proverbs 17:22 NIV).

But time marches on. I move a little farther down the road. One out of one dies. Death, especially my own death, isn't a laughing matter.

The brow furrows. There is a pursing of the lips and a tearing of the eye. My body, once strong and durable, is becoming weak and fragile. Mentally, I used to be sharp and alert, and now I'm becoming dull and forgetful. I can't do what I used to do, quickly and easily. My joints are becoming stiff. I move slowly. The bounce in my step is gone.

My tennis racket is resting on the closet shelf beside a canister of unopened balls. A pair of New Balance running shoes sits in my closet, barely broken in. Didn't I start that book three months ago? But I never finished it. Sometimes I just sit and stare out the window until I fall asleep in the chair. And I know what is happening.

I miss half of the table conversation. The other half probably wasn't worth hearing, or so I tell myself. It was good to get a note from my granddaughter, taking a few minutes for old Grandpa Randy. She's really thoughtful. Comes from good stock, and it shows.

Yes, I think it's time to go on hospice. The doctor said the tumor is growing, and the cancer has probably spread. I'm not a candidate for surgery. I don't think I want to go through the chemo or the radiation treatments, not at my age.

The end is getting closer every day, one day closer to my Father's home.

And I ask myself, "So Chaplain Randy, how do you live when the end is getting closer?" And the answer I give myself is this: "The same way I would live if I didn't have a tumor and I could still bound from here to there and play three sets of tennis and carry my end of the conversation, doing as much as I can as well as I can for as long as I can." But I know it will soon be different. *Much* is becoming less, and *long* is getting shorter.

Jesus is the one who would tell me, "Randy, you have nothing to prove. You have nothing to hide. You have nothing to lose. Just live with wonder, love, and praise. Just live with contentment, joy, and peace. Live the life of a servant - faithfully, confidently, and hopefully. I am coming soon!"

Can life become burdensome? Of course it can. Can I grow weary of the journey—more doctors, more prescriptions, more limitations, more loneliness, more angst, more discouragement, more grief, and more pain? *Yes, I can!*

Does there come a time, like an approaching storm front moving slowly from the west to the east, a time when life on this side of eternity begins to lose its zest, its spark, its vitality, even its meaning? Yes, it can happen. It does happen. I've seen it happen. The faithful

Christian begins to identify more and more with the dogged determination of the apostle Paul.

Knowing full well that his rendezvous with a Roman executioner had been decreed by the Emperor Nero, Paul wrote to Timothy from prison and declared, "I have fought the good fight, I have finished the race, I have kept the faith. Now there is in store for me the crown of righteousness, which the Lord, the righteous Judge, will award to me on that day—and not only to me, but also to all who have longed for his appearing" (2 Timothy 4:7–8 NIV).

I have watched many of my friends over the years come to this point. They were not contemplating suicide. They were not psychologically unbalanced. They were not malcontents. They were just tired, weary of the journey. A new season of *American Idol* would not rekindle a fire in them. Friday afternoon bingo would not make their day. Another scenic ride to watch the eagles nesting along the Missouri River would not spark interest in the world around them. They were ready to die. They wanted to die.

Theologically speaking, death is my enemy. But the enemy has been defeated. Through faith in Christ there is life forever! St. Paul wrote, "Death has been swallowed up in victory. Where, O death is your victory? Where, O death is your sting. The sting of death is sin, and the power of sin is the law. But thanks be to God! He gives us the victory through our Lord Jesus Christ" (1 Corinthians 15:54–56 NIV).

It is not wrong to want to die. It is not wrong to pray, "I am ready to be with you, Lord. I want to live forever in the place you have prepared for me and all believers in Christ. Lord, take me home." At age eighty-five Margaret was ready. Margaret prayed to die. Margaret prayed, "Lord, Thy will be done."

Margaret's Story

Margaret and her husband, Earl, who had been married for more than fifty years, had planned carefully. They were going to move into an independent living apartment at Hidden Lake, and they were looking forward to it. But a week before the moving date she fell and broke her hip. She had surgery to repair the fracture, followed by physical therapy in our care center. Her goal was to walk again. When Margaret entered the care center, Earl went ahead and moved into their independent living apartment. Assuming that her therapy would go well, he expected Margaret to join him very soon, and so did she.

But at some point during this whole process, a series of health complications flooded into Margaret's life like a dam that had burst. She was hospitalized for more than two weeks. Things did not go well for her. She was diagnosed with congestive heart failure, pneumonia, and renal failure. Her body was seriously compromised. Doctors were able to stabilize her with medications and to stem the decreasing function of her kidneys with dialysis. Three times a week she would undergo a four-hour dialysis procedure. The procedure essentially recycled her blood, removing the chemical impurities (poisons) that the kidneys were not removing.

And then very unexpectedly things went from bad to worse. While Margaret was dealing with her issues, Earl had been diagnosed with pancreatic cancer. By the time the doctors had discovered the cancer, it had already spread throughout his body. Electing not to undergo any kind of invasive procedure, Earl died in less than a month. Is this beginning to sound like a modern-day version of the Job narrative? Here's the rest of the story.

Margaret was a remarkable Christian. She had a strong faith in her Savior, Jesus, and she wore that faith on her sleeve. She was a talker, a people person, just a delight to be around. I never heard a word of complaint about her declining health. She did not rue the day she fell and broke her hip, as though it might have been the catalyst to the even more serious health issues she was now facing. She did not question God's goodness. She did not waver in her love for Him. She knew he had first loved her. She knew that Christ was her solid rock and that all other ground was sinking sand.

Margaret was a living testimony to the saving work of Jesus Christ, God's only Son and her only Savior. His faithfulness to her and to her family (two married sons and several grandchildren) was never in doubt. The time that I spent at her bedside was like receiving an infusion of spiritual adrenalin. I never left her room feeling sad but always left feeling pumped up. Margaret *preached* the Gospel to me as few pulpit preachers ever have. Her life beamed with hope!

But Margaret was dying, and she knew it. After only a few weeks on dialysis, she made an informed decision. No more dialysis. Would she be taking her own life? No. Yet by taking herself off dialysis, the end point of her death was sure to come sooner, and she knew that. She was ready to die. She was more than ready. Her heartfelt desire was to depart and to be with Christ. This became her simple and singular prayer: "Lord Jesus, take me home to be with you!"

Less than six weeks after Earl had died, Margaret died. Her family was in the room, encircling her bed. I had gotten the call from the nurses' station that she was actively dying. When I stepped into the room, I was grateful that I already had a relationship with this family. We exchanged greetings. There was the quiet conversation of recall. It had been just over a month ago that we had all been together at Christian Hospital Northeast, gathered in Earl's room, as his life slipped away. Now it was happening again.

I never know exactly what I'm going to say at a time like this. There is no script to follow, and it's not preach-a-sermon time.

No script means that I must let the Holy Spirit nudge or push or shove or restrain or make clear. The Holy Spirit is good at doing all of that and much more! No script means letting the moment unfold, letting God be God, and not getting in His way. No script means that sometimes I say very little.

As I stood at the foot of Margaret's bed, her breathing noticeably shallow, I remembered what I had read earlier that morning in my quiet time, my devotional time. "Into your hands I commit my spirit; you have redeemed me, O Lord, faithful God" (Psalm 31:5 RSV).

Softly I shared those words, connecting them with the words of Jesus, His prayer from the cross just before He died. Seconds later Margaret peacefully breathed her last breath. The spirit left her body. She was dead.

I had been in the room for no more than two or three minutes. A quiet hush settled in—the kind of stillness that begs description, moments that cannot be measured by time. Serenity swept over the room. And then there were tears. Healthy, necessary grieving began. Husbands and wives embraced. After the first wave of emotion subsided, I prayed with them and for them. With a brief, parting word of pastoral care, I stepped away from their holy ground.

I left the room to tell the nurse that Margaret had died, recalling the hymn verse, "Though we sow in tears of sorrow, we shall reap in heavenly joy."

Sometimes I cry. Sometimes I groan inside. Sometimes the groan comes to my lips. Sometimes I am numb. Sometimes it hits me later. Sometimes I am left drained and just need to be alone. Sometimes I feel a sense of holy joy and could break out into a chorus of "When the Saints Go Marching in!" Every death is different. But my prayer at the end of each day remains the same.

I learned this prayer as a child. Maybe you did too. My parents taught it to me and to my sisters. It was part of our bedtime prayers, together as a family. I taught it to my children and prayed it with them at their bedsides countless times. And their father continues to pray it like a child at the end of his day: "Now I lay me down to sleep. I pray Thee, Lord, my soul to keep. If I should die before I wake, I pray Thee, Lord, my soul to take. If I should live another day, I pray Thee, Lord, to guide my way. And this I ask for Jesus' sake. Amen."

Today the Hidden Lake flag is at full mast.

CHAPTER 13

A Final Reflection

I write a monthly article for our newsletter titled "Chaplain Randy's Reflection." In it I share myself. I share my ministry. Over the years I have become more transparent, roaming the waterfront of my thoughts and feelings and experiences, sometimes seriously and other times humorously.

I do not use my reflection as a bully pulpit. I do not craft it as a straightforward devotional piece. I write in order to connect with our residents and with their families by offering up a thin slice of everyday life—God at work in the ordinary, and God at work in my life. The spiritual person that I am (that we all are) is part of the ordinary.

Recently the article came out like this – a blend of poetic free-verse, images captured, thoughts shared, experiences recalled; reflection refined, and all of this opened a window to my soul:

> Reflection—as in sunlight glistening off a snow
> covered slope, so bright it hurts the eyes, unprotected
> by dark glasses.

Reflection—as in moonlight, shining off a quiet lake, a soft brightness that bathes the night in warm hues of blue and grey.

Reflection—as in a photograph, an image frozen in time: "This is how I looked then. This is where I was then," looking back on a captured moment.

Reflection—as in a mirror, looking at myself—"So this is what others see when they look at me. Mirrors do not lie. I guess I could use a haircut."

Reflection—as in a conversation, stepping back, recalling how it was, laughing or crying, life already lived—some down time for bringing the past into perspective.

Reflection—as in time alone, sifting through my thoughts, wondering and waiting—conversing silently with God, listening to His still small voice, and so peaceful.

Reflection—as in Chaplain Randy's, a boy from the farm in Kansas, a cherished childhood, still getting lost in the city, still a child in many ways, a boy not yet grown up.

Reflection—as in Chaplain Randy's, a position—sometimes lonely, a calling not sought after but conferred, an opportunity to serve others, in Jesus' Name.

Reflection—as in Chaplain Randy's, a collection of personal thoughts printed on a page, and shared with readers, some unknown. Worth reading? Maybe. Maybe not.

Reflection—as in spiritual truth, the Scriptures—definitely worth reading and learning and applying. Remember, Gospel Teaching on Thursday at 1:00—an hour well spent.

Reflection—as in Jesus on the cross, the climax of his ministry. He looks back. He lives in the present. He reaches to the future: "Father, forgive them!" *Grace!*

Reflection—as on that morning, when an angel announced to women at the tomb: "He (Jesus) is not here; he has risen!" The best Good News for you and me!

This book has been a collage of reflections.

Eight months after becoming the chaplain at Hidden Lake, my mother died. The cause of death was a form of coronary obstruction pulmonary disease (COPD). She had lived with it and had received treatment for it during the last ten years of her life. On May 3, 2003, her seventy-six years of earthly life ended.

In late July 2009 my father had a stroke. He became a care center resident at a facility in St. Joseph, MO. He recovered sufficiently to move into an assisted living facility for seven months. In November of 2010 his brain hemorrhaged again. Seventeen days later he died, two days before his eighty-sixth birthday.

My mother was twenty, and my dad was twenty-two when I was born. As a child, I never imagined my parents becoming old, becoming weak, and becoming frail. As I was aging, so were they. I always thought my mother would live longer than she did. (Her grandfather had lived to be ninety-four). I had hoped my father could always live independently. I can remember hearing him say, "I never want to live in a nursing home." But that's where he died.

Again and again the lesson must be retaught and relearned. We have no control. We never know how it's going to be. We have no clue how it's going to end.

My sisters and I have grown closer, dealing with the loss of our mother, attending to our dad through changing times and his eventual death. Jan, the nurse, Kris, the teacher, and Randy, the chaplain—we were a team! We trusted one another, communicated with one another, cared for one another, and loved our parents dearly. The cooperative spirit, none of us living close to our home of origin, was huge, was critical, and was always there. We shed our tears, but there was laughter too. Sometimes we could only shake our heads, shrug our shoulders, and say, "It is what it is. But with the Lord, we'll get through this." And we did.

Having watched my dad age, watching my resident-friends age, and ministering to the forgetful, the repetitious, the disgruntled, or those whose faces have become blank stares, I keep coming back to this and reminding myself of this: *As I am, so they once were. As they are, so I will be.*

I am still learning what it means to provide pastoral care. It is not a science. It is not an art form. Pastoral care has become for me a way of life.

I am a professional with a professional sense of pride in what I do. I have a professional title—chaplain. I am in a professional position as a caregiver. There are professional expectations that others have of me and that I have of myself. There are professional responsibilities that have been entrusted to me. There are professional decisions that I must make, alone or collaborating with others. There are professional presentations that I routinely make. At the end of the day I am a professional, and I am reimbursed for my services.

It's all very professional—Rev. Dr. Randall Shields, Lutheran Senior Services chaplain, serving residents at the community of Hidden Lake. But strip all of that professional stuff away, and what lies beneath the surface? What makes pastoral care my way of life?

Jesus said, "I came not to be served, but to serve, and to give my life as a ransom for many" (Mark 10:45 NIV). This is where pastoral care begins—the mystery and the reality that I have been loved, served, ransomed.

I bring nothing to the table. I have no resume to impress. Jesus simply loves me! Jesus has given extraordinary value to my life! Jesus has served me with His life! Jesus knows all about me, and He loves me just the same. Jesus knows that I am selfish, that I am hypocritical, that I am rigid, stubborn, and intolerant. I look out for number one, pretending that I am number one. I am impatient and restless. I have a need to be right, even when I am wrong, and Jesus knows all of that, all of my sin.

Sometimes I simply get by, donning my professional hat, putting on my professional face, using my professional jargon, and doing my professional thing.

Professional care can become a business. Professional facades can disguise a gutless functionary. How unsettling honesty can be. How painful transparency and confession can be. But how redemptive and restorative the Gospel can be!

Jesus takes frail flesh. Jesus takes frail flesh and dies. Jesus takes frail flesh and dies for me. Jesus makes all the difference!

What is underneath my professional caregiving veneer? God in Christ at work: my bruised and broken heart - loved and cared for; my raw and anguished spirit - gently embraced and tenderly healed. I am a cracked pot - fully restored. I am a forgiven sinner - graciously received.

Slowly but surely, I am absorbing the title of Henri Nouwen's book *The Wounded Healer*. I am more able to feel the hurt and pain of others, because it is my own hurt and pain. I can more readily feel the loss and loneliness of others because of my own loss and because I, too, have been lonely.

I am more sensitive to the anger and to the frustration of others because I have been there, and I still go there. I can more easily grieve with others, for I, too, have grieved … and still grieve.

Jesus says, "Serve, as I have served you. Give, as I have given unto you. Love, as I have loved you. Touch, as I have touched you. Comfort, as I have comforted you. Embrace, as I have embraced you. Die to yourself, as I have died for you."

What have I discovered underneath my professional title and position? I am simply an amateur—nothing more than an amateur. An amateur is still learning. An amateur is teachable and approachable. An amateur is a work in progress. An amateur makes mistakes and then turns them into a growing experience. An amateur is not in it for the money. An amateur is not on the clock. An amateur is not credentialed and registered and recognized.

An amateur, as the root meaning of the word in Latin would remind us, is someone who does something *simply because he or she loves to do it*. It has become his or her passion!

Amateur caregivers do need to be gifted in order to serve effectively. Amateur caregivers do need to be equipped in order to serve faithfully. Amateur caregivers will want to be trained in order to better serve. Amateur caregivers will want to be mentored by experienced caregivers. And professional caregivers will want to hone and fine-tune their skills so that with all the zeal of an amateur, they too can more effectively meet the needs of others.

I am a professional, who is an amateur caregiver at heart. I am an amateur, who has been called to be a chaplain, the position of a professional caregiver.

I have never had a more fulfilling ministry than I have now, serving the residents of Hidden Lake and serving with a management team, committed to helping older adults live life to the fullest. In the context of this ministry I have also been greatly loved, accepted, and cared for. It is the ebb and flow of a faith-based community.

At a time when my marital life had gone through upheaval (the stress of separation and then divorce), I experienced refuge without judgment. I became a resident at Hidden Lake. This is my home. I am part of the community. The residents have become my extended family, and many of them have drawn me into theirs.

The day I told the residents I was moving and would become their neighbor is a day vividly etched into my memory. I could not tell everyone in person, but I knew if I told a select few, then word would get around. So as my Thursday afternoon Gospel Teaching class came to an end, I used that moment with those faithful folks to become very personal. What followed could best be described by the expression "stunned silence."

I stretched my transparency that day nearly to the breaking point. I exposed my marital failure. I owned the wrong. I confessed my sin.

Divorce snuffs out God's design for marriage. I shared the thunder and the rumble of that painful truth. And I held tenaciously to the Gospel words of Jesus, "Take heart, my son, your sins have been forgiven" (Matthew 9:2 RSV). As I ended, I said with quivering voice, "So now I'm showing you how scarred with human failure your chaplain is."

Immediately Grace raised her hand to speak and said, "Randy, we have seen how human you are for as long as you have been here, and that's why we love you."

My eyes welled with tears. Grace had shared her name with me!

Every beginning has an ending. I do not know when, but some day this ministry will end. I will grieve the loss that comes with an ending, and I will give thanks for the journey that I have been on. The mantle of caring will pass to another. The residents of Hidden Lake will be served by another chaplain, one as able, or more able than I am.

Ministry was happening here before I came. Ministry will be happening here after I leave. I know I am replaceable.

My friend Grace, who had graced me that particular afternoon in my Gospel Teaching class, came to my office several months prior to this. It was Pastor Appreciation Month. She had come to tell me face-to-face, rather than with a card, how much she valued my ministry.

Grace talked for at least twenty minutes, not in glittering generalities; she focused on specific aspects of this ministry. I have to say that she made me feel very good about myself and affirmed the way I was doing ministry at Hidden Lake. As she got up and moved toward the door, she paused, and then said, "Randy, I hope you don't leave before I die."

Others along the way have expressed a similar kind of sentiment. "When I die, I want you to do my funeral." I have honored some of those requests, and some are still outstanding. I consider this to be the consummate compliment for any chaplain serving in a retirement community like Hidden Lake.

The residents have been my teachers. This is what I have learned. It is neither profound nor original, but nonetheless I pass it on to you. Tell people and show people *today* how much you care about them and love them. Tomorrow they may not understand; tomorrow they may not be here.

EPILOGUE

Has it been an age appropriate book? Are you an age appropriate reader? (Do you recall the preface?) For this reflective chaplain, it all comes down to this: In Christ Jesus, live *faithfully, even* as you age *gracefully,* until you die *peacefully,* and then live *eternally* with Jesus Christ!

Between now and then, may the testimony of the psalmist punctuate all of our days. "Since my youth, O God, you have taught me, and to this day I declare your marvelous deeds. Even when I am old and gray, do not forsake me, O God, till I declare your power to the next generation, your might to all who are to come" (Psalm 71:17–18 NIV).

CPSIA information can be obtained at www.ICGtesting.com
Printed in the USA
LVOW12s2317061014

407490LV00002B/4/P

9 781462 738434